LET'S DANCE

LET'S DANCE

The Complete Book and DVD of Ballroom Dance Instruction for Weddings, Parties, Fitness, and Fun

DANCE LIKE *A* STAR IN MINUTES

Including the Basics for the Foxtrot, Waltz, Swing, Salsa, Merengue, and Line Dances

Created by **Cal Pozo**

Foreword by Pierre Dulaine

Photos by Peter Field Peck

HATHERLEIGH PRESS

NEW YORK

Hatherleigh Press

5-22 46th Avenue, Suite 200

Long Island City, NY 11101

www.hatherleighpress.com

Library of Congress Cataloging-in-Publication Data

Pozo, Cal

Let's Dance/Cal Pozo.

    p.cm.

ISBN 978-1-57826-241-0

1. Ballroom dancing--Handbooks, manuals, etc.

2. Dance--Handbooks, manuals, etc. I. Title.

GV1751.D43 2007

793.3'3--dc22

                    2007004938

ISBN 978-1-57826-241-0

Let's Dance is available for bulk purchase, special promotions, and premiums. For information on reselling and special purchase opportunities, call 1-800-528-2550 and ask for the Special Sales Manager.

Interior design by Allison Furrer, Jasmine Cardoza, Deborah Miller

Cover design by Deborah Miller

10 9 8 7 6 5 4 3 2 1

Printed in United States

Acknowledgments

Every creative concept I've been part of required the contribution and passion of a lot of people. The process of getting this book and DVD produced and released is no exception. And whereas acknowledging and thanking every single person who has helped me bring this project to fruition—graphic designers, photographers, audio/video production crews, musical composers, the wonderful staff at Hatherleigh Press, the book's models—would end up in too long a list, there are a few among them to whom I must extend my heartfelt gratitude:

My editor, Andrea Au, whose vision and patience has guided me through every step in this process, and her staff at Hatherleigh Press, including Deborah Miller, Alyssa Smith, Jasmine Cardoza, and Allison Furrer.

My friend, Pierre Dulaine, and the staff of his American Ballroom Theatre Dance Studio, especially Vanessa Villalobos, who was as great a teacher as she was a source of information;

My assistant, Doug Pawliuk, whose friendship and help will always be appreciated.

Last, but certainly not least, I must give a very special thank you to:

My two dance partners featured in the DVD, Luba Feldman and Nicole Dowell, with whom I wish I could go out dancing every night;

Our models for the book, Nicholas Atkinson, Sara Lukasiewicz, Robert A. Pennacchia, and Claire Tobin.

Robert Peterson, whose creative and technical genius are evident in the editing of this program's DVD.

And to Jean Hurkin-Torres, whose love for dance, editing talents, and eye for detail has made it all possible.

Dedication

To Eugene "Luigi" Facciuto
Friend, Teacher, Inspiration

Contents

Foreword by Pierre Dulaine

In the movie *Take the Lead*, Antonio Banderas plays the role of a dance instructor who volunteers to teach ballroom dancing at a New York City public school to an unlikely group of hip-hop-loving high school students. In the Oscar-nominated documentary film, *Mad Hot Ballroom*, a group of New York City fourth and fifth-graders experience a similar situation. Both films are based on a true life story. Mine.

When I first got into a New York City public school to start a ten-week ballroom dance class, I knew that the kids I was about to meet had no real idea of what it took for two people to dance as one, or of the process involved in making that happen.

I also knew that regardless of their individual ages, learning capabilities, and motivation, I needed to gain their confidence within the first minutes of that first dance class. If I didn't, there was a good chance that many would drop out.

Over the years, I have also worked with hundreds of couples seeking to learn how to dance at their wedding. Just like with my kids, most of these couples came to their first lesson with little or no idea of the time it would take them to learn how to dance to their "favorite song" or to learn the latest Latin dances. And just like with my kids, if within the first few minutes of our first class, I haven't been able to judge their learning potential, to relate to the immediacy of their needs, and to make what can be a stressful moment into a fun one, chances are they, too, will drop out.

Learning to dance is not difficult, especially learning the steps and moves of social level ballroom dancing. It is practically the same thing as walking to music. However, it does take a certain amount of dedication and time. When couples start planning their wedding party—locations, halls, caterers, flowers, photographers, invitations—they generally do so months in advance of their big night. Dancing lessons, on the other hand, are too often left for the last minute.

In this book, Cal admits that "a book or video cannot match what you can learn from private instruction." I agree. Yet I have often wished that brides and grooms would do a little homework before they come to me for lessons. This book is just the thing they need to prepare.

If you are a bride or groom to be and are reading this book, congratulations! The information Cal has compiled will help you pick the right song and dance for you to dance at your wedding—and give you the instruction you need to do it well. The book and the DVD work hand-in-hand, providing simple and easy-to-follow textual and visual dance instruction. If you seek private instruction after you read this book, you will be starting with an all-around solid base that will save you lots of time and money. If you've already taken a few private lessons, this book will refresh your memory and help you refine your technique and add a few picture-perfect moves.

Finally, here are a few pointers I have learned from my students that will help you make your first dance less stressful and much more memorable:

1. Don't think of your first dance as a performance. Think of it as a symbolic gesture, as if starting your new life by dancing on the correct foot. It is a metaphor of your new life encapsulated in the three minutes of that song's duration. It is a gift you are presenting to your friends and family, something that brings them into your experience.

2. Be aware that sometimes a song that has a romantic meaning to the two of you may be too rich in lyrics to be danced to. Have more than one choice. Discuss your selections with your dance instructor and with the DJ or band who is going to be in charge of your musical entertainment.

3. If you have hired a band and are planning to have it play your selected song, do not hesitate to find out if they have played it before. If they haven't and you don't want to take a chance, find out if they have recorded live performances of other popular wedding songs and ask to listen to them. You'll be surprised at how different a song recorded on a CD will sound when played live.

4. If you are considering sharing the spotlight with one of your parents, even for a brief dance, don't wait until the last minute to rehearse with them or to seek an instructor that can coach both of you. Remember, the eyes—and camera lenses—of lots of people are going to be honed on you.

Learning to dance should be a pleasant journey. It is in that journey where the true joy of dancing is found and not in the final results.

Enjoy!

Pierre Dulaine
American Ballroom Theater

Introduction

To many people even the idea of dancing, especially with a partner, is intimidating. Yet dancing has been a part of our lives even before we're born. While still in our mother's womb, we are constantly reacting to the beat of her heart. Whenever she moves or changes body positions, we frequently respond by adjusting ours. Then, long before our eyes open or focus, our nervous system is commanding our legs and arms to respond to sounds and movements it continues to perceive internally and externally.

As our vision clears and we can make out the images of those who whistle, sing or baby talk to us, what do we do? We shake our limbs, we bob our heads, roll our eyes. We dance!

There are many different forms and styles of dance. All of them share two common elements. One is a physical reaction to music we enjoy listening to. The other is the use of the body as a tool to communicate that enjoyment. When two people are able to merge those two common elements while following a sequence of predetermined steps and moves, they're forming a rhythmic partnership. They are partner dancing.

There are various forms of partner dancing. Each has its own levels of proficiency. Social dancing is the first level of what is traditionally known as ballroom dancing. Not all traditional ballroom dances fit into a social mode. Some need a lot of space to be danced correctly, something you won't find in most nightclubs or halls where weddings and other parties might be held. If after reading this book, you become inspired to go beyond the social level, you'll have all the ingredients you need, because the fundamental elements are the same in social and competitive ballroom dance.

Personally, I'm thrilled to have the opportunity to bring dance into people's lives. Dance has been a part of my entire life. My own first dance lesson took place when I was about ten years old in Havana, Cuba, my native country. My teacher was my family's best dancer, my father. At parties he was often called "the mambo dancer." The many times I watched him dance with my mother remain the most memorable moments of my childhood. In much later years, when my parents would come to see me perform on stage or in ballroom dance competitions, they never ceased to give me pointers. Although I had progressed beyond the social level of dance, they were still the masters; they had the ability to communicate and express each other's love for dance on the floor, the ability to have fun dancing even if all you know is a couple of steps. That ability is what distinguishes a good dance partner from an unforgettable one.

Once you achieve that sense of communication between you and your dance partner, you'll never want to stop learning more steps, techniques, and styles. Everything you'll find in this book and its DVD is designed to get you started, to get your mind and body to think, "Let's dance." But my real objective is to get you hooked on dancing because I know that once you know you can dance, you'll want to continue learning. You'll never stop dancing.

Thank you for the opportunity.

Let's dance.

Cal Pozo
www.calpozo.com

About Partner Dancing

During the first half of the last century, people flocked to dance halls and hotel ballrooms that headlined dance orchestras and bandleaders like Benny Goodman, Duke Ellington, Glenn Miller and the Dorsey brothers. Back then these master pioneers of jazz and swing music were as much of a celebrity as many of today's top singing stars, their music being played over and over on radio stations. Around the start of the century's second half, musical styles and social dancing in America started to experience a progression of significant changes due to the advent of rock and roll.

Although seasoned dancers could still swing-dance to many rock and roll tunes, "rock dances" were danced without partners touching each other or even mirroring the same moves. The upside of this was that more people took to dance floors than ever before because anyone could dance by just "doing their own thing." The downside was that partner dancing, two people dancing as one, retreated to a handful of night-clubs, ballroom dance halls, and dance studios.

During the sixties, an offshoot of rock and roll dancing started to become popular. Instead of dancers facing each other or dancing around each other, they stood side-by-side forming long parallel lines and dancing to songs and melodies with innovative, sometimes odd, titles like the Pony, the Watusi, the Madison, the Mashed Potato, the Monkey, the Stroll, and many others. Yet these were dances that followed a choreographed pattern that not everyone could follow. It would not be until the late sixties that the dance scene would again see huge amounts of people doing their own thing to one of that time's biggest hits—Chubby Checker's The Peppermint Twist.

During the early seventies, the dance scene experienced an even greater change. The catalyst was the beat of a newly released song and the sound of the man who sang it. The song was the theme from the movie *Shaft*. The singer was Isaac Hayes. Both are frequently credited as having started the disco era of music and dance.

Around the same time as disco was becoming popular, a style of ballroom dancing that had already been quite popular in England started to make its way to the United States. Originally known as the English style, but presently known as the International style, it shared many of the same ballroom dances and characteristic steps of the American ballroom style. But it established more structured techniques in footwork, dance positions, and complexity of dance for ballroom dance patterns, all of which created a set of technical and performing standards that are still followed to this day worldwide.

Today, ballroom dancers frequently integrate steps and moves from both the American and the International style into their dancing. This fusion of styles is also present in the routines danced in hit TV shows like *Dancing With the Stars* and *So You Think You Can Dance*. However, at officially sanctioned competitions, dancers remain true to the patterns and techniques of their dance style or category.

In *Dancing With the Stars*, for which I recently directed and choreographed a DVD featuring ballroom dance moves viewers can do without a partner for exercise and weight loss, professional ballroom instructors are paired with media celebrities who have had no previous ballroom dance training. Undoubtedly, this show has brought ballroom dancing into more homes worldwide than, possibly, even DVD versions of the movies of Fred Astaire and Ginger Rogers. This show has also achieved something no other dance-based television show, Broadway musical, or movie has been able to. It has proven that with dedication, time and, yes, a lot of effort, even professional football players can become amazingly good ballroom dancers, winning not only a top prize but also the admiration and respect of an enormous viewing audience.

In other words, anyone can learn to dance—and dance well—even if you think you may have "no rhythm," "two left feet," "no coordination," or too busy a schedule.

Categories of Ballroom Dance

The American ballroom dance style lends itself more to a social level of dancing; it is much easier to learn and to perform in a shorter period of time. Dances in the American style are grouped into two major categories: smooth dances and rhythm dances.

On the dance floor, smooth dances—including the foxtrot, waltz, and tango—move in a counter-clockwise direction. These dances require that partners stay in close body contact or "closed dance position," and in a firmly maintained, upright, body posture. Smooth dances are characterized by long, gliding strides that combine quick and slow foot movements.

There are two different groups of rhythm dances: American and Latin. The American rhythm dances are the lindy/swing and the hustle, both of U.S. origin. The Latin dances are the salsa/mambo, the rumba, the slow rumba (bolero) and the cha-cha, all of Cuban origin. Just as popular is the merengue, a dance of Dominican origin. The Brazilian samba, a popular dance among competitive ballroom dancers, is not played at most parties or weddings, so I have not included it in this book. At a social level, most rhythm dances do not move around or across a dance floor. The distance between foot movements is short, generally about shoulder-width apart, and the steps are danced in a relatively small space, allowing the torso, rib cage, hips and knees to move with more freedom and pizzazz. In rhythm dances partners move in and out from a variety of dance positions.

In the International style the smooth dances are the slow foxtrot, the waltz, the tango, the quickstep and the Viennese Waltz. All are dances that call for close body contact throughout with partners maintaining an elegantly erect posture and a firm dance position hold commonly referred to as the "dance frame."

The Latin dances in the International style are the rumba, the cha-cha and the samba. All three are danced at a faster tempo than in the American style. The paso doble is a dance fashioned after the stately march that matadors perform when entering the bullfighting ring. In the pasodoble, the male represents the matador while the female represents the matador's cape.

The jive is the last dance in International style competitions. The jive does resemble the American style lindy/hop, which is the original swing, but International style dancers perform the jive at a much faster tempo. It is quite a showy and athletic dance, requiring tremendous stamina and a strong cardiovascular system. That's why it's the last dance performed in a competition's rhythm division. After two minutes of jiving, water and a chair frequently follow.

Today, ballroom dancing is experiencing something of a comeback. Yet ballroom dancing had not gone away nor ever will. Throughout the United States, ballroom dance competitions have been held at the local, regional and national level for many years. Salsa, swing, and line dance competitions often fill hotel ballrooms on a weekly basis. And if the success of the documentary *Mad Hot Ballroom*, based on the life and work of my longtime friend, Pierre Dulaine, featuring New York City kids dancing and competing in ballroom dances, is a sign of the future, I see huge dance halls and great dance orchestras in the not too distant future coming back as well.

If that does happen, you'll be ready.

Dancing at Wedding and Parties

It is quite the norm for a bride and groom to discuss the songs and tunes they want to hear at their wedding with either the DJ or with the orchestra leader they've hired. People hosting parties, especially parties with a given theme or objective—charities, award cere-monies and other similar galas—often assign someone to make a list of songs and tunes, according to the occasion as well as to the average age of those who will be attending. If you are involved in the music's planning, and you'd like to show off your dance talents with a couple of salsa or swing steps, all you need to do is convey your wishes. If you're an invited guest, you won't be frowned at if you ask the DJ or the orchestra if they have a rumba or a cha-cha (but never a tango) they could play. If the answer is yes, you should still ask your host if it is OK for your request to be fulfilled— even if the host is your brother, sister, or cousin. You may be very surprised at how many people will end up sharing the dance floor with you.

Over the years, I've known a lot of couples who got bitten by the ballroom dance bug after taking a few lessons at a dance studio in preparation for their wedding. Just about any dance studio in your area will advertise a "wedding package." Generally, this package consists of a group of one-on-one lessons during which you'll probably be taught some beginning level steps in dances like the waltz and the foxtrot as well as dances many studios refer to as "nightclub dances." These range from free-style pop dancing to some basic swing.

If you are among the many who are now planning their wedding and have discussed taking some private dance instruction (which I must admit can never be matched by what you learn from a book or video), you will find that what you've learned in this book will help you advance your learning a lot faster, and maybe even save you a few bucks.

To make your dance lessons even more effective, here are a few tips.

1. Make a list of songs and tunes you and your love would like to dance to as your "first

Here's a list of some of the most popular traditional ballads played for the "first dance" and for the "father-daughter" dance.

FIRST DANCE

"Nothing Compares to You"
Sinead O'Connor

"From This Moment On"
Shania Twain

"Unforgetable"
Natalie Cole or Nat King Cole

"Circle of Life"
Elton John

"You Light Up My Life"
Debbie Boone

"The Way You Look Tonight"
Tony Bennett

FATHER-DAUGHER

"I Get a Kick Out of You"
Frank Sinatra

"Just in Time"
Tony Bennett

"Fly Me to the Moon"
Frank Sinatra

"Sunrise, Sunset"
Perry Como

"Could I Have This Dance"
Anne Murray

dance" as husband and wife. Most people make this selection based on the lyrics of songs they both like and that have some special meaning to both. Hence the reason why most "first dances" are love ballads.

2. Take your list to your dance instructor. Many ballads have melodies and rhythmical changes that don't exactly lend themselves to couples keeping a steady beat while dancing. Remember, all eyes will be on both of you. And some ballads are too long. Three minutes should be about the maximum time of your first dance. Remember, guests have come to your wedding to celebrate the occasion with you, but also to eat and drink.

3. What both of you will be wearing should also be considered in your selection of a dance. For the bride, a floor-length wedding gown, especially those with a train, will limit not only the dances that can be done, but also the steps. For example, dance patterns that travel forward or backward present an open invitation for the shoes of either the groom or the bride to step on the dress's hemline. It is for that reason that when wearing a floor-length wedding gown, ballads are the best tunes to dance to and the signature dance patterns of the foxtrot or the waltz (both featured in this book) are always the safest choice for either the first dance or the father-and-daughter dance.

I have attended a few weddings where the bride changes into a shorter dress after the cake is cut. This is a smart thing to do if budget allows, and one that will allow you to dance with all the guests without fear of ruining a beautiful wedding gown.

For the groom, there are a lot of dance choices. However, whether you are wearing a new suit or a more formal tuxedo suit, make sure that its fit allows you to raise your elbows up and out to the sides of your body without the jacket's collar rising beyond your ears. Often, a wonderful-looking suit that's fit while you're standing still makes an awful-looking photograph if taken while you're on the dance floor.

How to Use This Book

Let's Dance provides you with several learning tools, including textual information and instruction, photographs, diagrams of dance patterns, and one-on-one DVD tutorials.

Let's Dance is divided into four main parts each containing a number of chapters.

In Part One, each chapter details one of the fundamental elements of partner dancing: footwork, timing and rhythm, dance positions, pattern building blocks, and individual characteristics. Reading through them should take you just a few minutes, but the information will provide you with a solid partner dancing foundation that will expedite your learning the dance patterns of the dance or dances that you are most interested in learning first.

In Part Two, The Smooth Dances, chapters focus on the foxtrot, the waltz and the tango.

In Part Three, The Latin Rhythm Dances, chapters focus on the salsa/mambo, the rumba, the cha-cha, and the merengue.

In Part Four, The American Rhythm Dances, chapters focus on the swing and the hustle.

In Part Five, Party and Line Dances, chapters focus on country line dances like the Boot Scootin'

Boogie and party line dances like the Electric Slide and the Macarena.

The dances featured under each of the five parts follow a three-step formula.

The Three-Step Formula

Obviously, there's a lot more to dancing with a partner than knowing what to do with your feet. There are a number of dance terms and techniques that apply to all dances, regardless of their level, and a number of additional ones that vary from level to level.

The dance terms and techniques that I've included in *Let's Dance* relate specifically to the dances and patterns found in this book. To further speed your learning, I've structured every chapter to follow a three-step formula. It consists of the Fundamentals Phase, the Dance Patterns Phase, and the Lead and Follow Phase.

THE FUNDAMENTALS PHASE

In this phase you'll learn all of the individual dance terms and technical components of your dance of choice. This phase requires little or no immediate physical interaction on your part. However, you'll find yourself reading and reviewing The Fundamental Phase that refers to your dance or dance style of choice several times before they're totally ingrained in your memory bank.

THE DANCE PATTERNS PHASE

This phase concentrates on the step-by-step, musical count-by-musical count and rhythm and foot placement (footwork and foot placement direction) of each of a dance's featured patterns.

Dance patterns follow an order starting with the dance's signature patterns and continuing on with other patterns that are either related to signature patterns or that you can link with signature patterns, thus ending up with a short dance routine. At parties some dances are more popular than others. I have therefore included more patterns in those dances than just their signature ones. Yet, overall, my selection of patterns has been made on the basis of their ease of execution and of lead and follow.

The breakdown of the fundamentals for each dance pattern will appear in the same format. Let's take a look at the foxtrot's Box Step as an example. First, you will see a box outlining the fundamentals of the Box Step.

> TIMING: 4/4
> RHYTHM: SQQ
> NUMBER OF COUNTS: 8
> NUMBER OF STEPS: 6
> CHARACTERISTICS: Longer forward and back steps than side steps. Whenever the moving foot "closes" next to the supporting foot, the body's weight immediately changes from the supporting foot over to the moving foot.

Then you will see a box listing each step of the dance pattern. In this example, we will show just the men's movements; the women's movements will appear in the same format on the opposite page.

Box	Step	Count	Rhythm	M—Foot Placement	DP
A	1	1 & 2	S	Fwd with LF	CL
	2	3	Q	Sd with RF	
	3	4	Q	Close LF to RF (WC)	
B	4	5 & 6	S	Bk with RF	
	5	7	Q	Sd with LF	
	6	8	Q	Close RF to LF (WC)	

The **Box** column will indicate which foot diagram this refers to.

The **Step** column indicates each foot placement. For example, Step 1 is your initial step and Step 3 is your third step.

The **Count** column indicates the number of musical beats taken per step.

The **Rhythm** column indicates the musical pace of the step: quick or slow.

The **M and W Foot Placement** columns indicate the foot you are to step with and the direction you are to take, for men and women, respectively.

The **DP** column indicates the Dance Position you are to maintain on every step you take.

Now, let's take a look at the footprint diagram of the Box Step. In this particular pattern, the entire pattern is shown in two boxed diagrams. Box A shows the first three foot placements (Steps 1 to 3) and their direction. Box B shows the three steps that follow (Steps 4 to 6) and their direction.

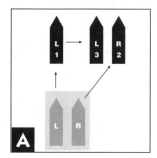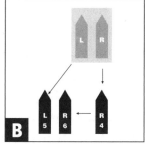

The Foxtrot—Box Step.

The starting positions of the Left and Right foot are shown in gray. Then the movement of each foot is shown in black. In each "footprint," you'll see a number, which corresponds to the foot placement indicated in the Step column. The arrows indicate the direction in which each moving foot needs to go. If you are stepping in place, that is denoted by a dotted line.

We've also included photographs that show either the step-by-step progression of a dance pattern, of a specific segment or move of a dance pattern, or of a sequence of movements that characterize that pattern or dance. For example, here are two photographs showing the difference between the Closed Dance Position (CL) and Dance Frame in the tango and the Closed Dance Position and Dance Frame in the rumba.

In addition, some dance patterns may require special pointers—Dance Tips—related to how best to lead or to follow steps or specific movements of

Tango
Closed Dance Position (CL).

Rumba
Closed Dance Position (CL).

that pattern. Some Dance Tips are written for either the man or the woman. Others are written for the attention of both.

THE LEAD AND FOLLOW PHASE

I call this your polishing phase for which there's nothing like watching the dance patterns being explained and danced live on your enclosed DVD. To do this I'm being assisted by two wonderful dancers, Luba Feldman and Nicole Dowell. We'll be showing you dance patterns at a speed that you can follow as well as dancing them to the music.

Sometimes, we focus our instruction on just one dance pattern at a time, especially when that pattern features special lead or follow techniques, or foot placement and moves that will need your special attention. Other times, we link two similar steps or variations of a basic step within one instructional segment. The DVD chapters vary in length. You will want to repeat some more times than others. All of them feature original musical compositions characteristic to the dance and composed at the best tempo for learning and practicing.

The featured patterns have been selected from my new *Partner Dancing 101 DVD* series.

How to Expedite Your Learning

Let's Dance covers a lot of material and instruction. However, the instructions follow a pyramid format with each piece of instruction acting as the foundation for the upcoming piece of instruction.

My suggestion is that you first concentrate on the dance or category of dance you are most interested in. For example, let's say that the first dance you're dying to learn is the salsa, today's most popular Latin dance. This is what I suggest you do.

1. Start by reading Part One. It gives you an overview of all the fundamental elements of partnered dances.

2. Next, go to Part Three, The Latin Rhythm Dances, where you will find additional information and instruction regarding Latin Dance Fundamentals.

3. Now you are ready for Chapter 10, The Salsa and the Mambo. Read through all the sections that deal with the fundamentals one more time: footwork, timing, dance positions, etc. Repetition is integral to memorization and to how fast you will learn and perform the steps.

4. Start with the first pattern. Look at the Footprint Diagram. Study it for a few seconds before trying it out.

5. Pop in the DVD. Click on Latin Dance Fundamentals and then on salsa. Select the first step: Forward and Back Breaks. Use your rewind or slow motion button to review. Repeat and practice.

Dance Terms and Abbreviations

All styles of dances have their own list of names, terms, and abbreviations that indicate everything from what the feet do and where they go to the positions of the body and the rhythms to which it moves. Frequently, different names are given to the same or similar dance patterns and dance moves.

In ballroom dance, sometimes the name of a particular step pattern, of an individual move, or of a sequence of individual steps changes according to the style of dance (International or American) or the category of a dance (smooth, Latin, or rhythm). For example, in International style dancing the American style "Fifth Position Break," a three-step sequence danced in the waltz as well as in the rumba is called a "Whisk." But the individual foot placement of the actual pattern is the same for both styles. Because this book features American style social-level patterns and techniques, the names I have given to the step patterns we feature are those generally used by most teachers of the American style.

Here's a list of terms and abbreviations as they appear in this book. Familiarize yourself with them as doing so will come in handy when following all textual instruction and information.

FOOTWORK AND FOOT PLACEMENT

HL: Heel Lead

BF: Ball/Flat

WF: Whole Foot

Fwd: Forward

Bk: Back

Sd: Side

TT: Toe Tap. The toe of one foot taps on the floor

Closed: The traveling foot steps next to the supporting foot and a change of weight takes place.

TIMING AND RHYTHM

4/4: Four musical counts or beats per group or measure of music

3/4: Three musical counts or beats per group or measure of music

2/4: Two musical counts or beats per group or measure of music

S: Slow Rhythm, meaning two counts of music per individual foot placement

Q: Quick Rhythm, meaning one count of music per individual foot placement

&: "and," meaning 1/2 a count of music per individual foot placement

DANCE POSITIONS (DP)

A: Apart

CL: Closed

LO: Left Open

LOD: Line of Dance

LS: Left Side

O: Open

RO: Right Open

RS: Right Side

UA: Underarm

DANCE HOLDS

1HH: One-Hand Hold

2HH: Two-Hand Hold

XHH: Cross-Hand Hold

BODY MOVEMENTS

WC: The body's weight changes from one foot to the other foot.

NWC: One foot is closing to the other foot, but no change of weight occurs.

CBM: Contra Body Motion

Pivots: A pivot is both a body movement and a foot action. The body rotates left or right while standing on one foot. Pivots range in movement between 1/4 to 1/2 turns.

Swivel: A swivel is also a body movement and a foot action. The body rotates left or right while standing on one or both feet. Swivels range in movement between 1/8 to 1/4 turns. A swivel can be done with just the heel, keeping the weight of the swiveling foot on the ball of that foot, or it can be done with just the toe, keeping the weight of the swiveling foot on the heel.

Hold: Body doesn't move from the position it has just reached.

DVD LESSON:

If I were to include in your DVD tutorial every piece of information that I have written up to this point, your bonus DVD would run longer than *Gone With the Wind*. You will therefore find that the DVD video instructions are focused on how to lead or follow the dance patterns featured in the book.

Most DVD chapters follow a formula. Instruction starts with the most basic, or signature, dance pattern then continues on with either a variation of that pattern or with an entirely different dance pattern.

Sometimes, depending on the complexity of the featured dance, I have chosen to breakdown just one dance pattern, teaching it first at a learning speed and then to the music. Other times, I have grouped two or three patterns into one lesson, ultimately linking them while performing them to music.

My choice of dance patterns and manner of instruction have the same objective: To provide you with an informal, and hopefully entertaining, way to turn your viewing area into your in-home dance studio—and to get you dancing with confidence in the shortest amount of time.

Part One
Fundamentals of Partner Dancing

All partner dances consist of predetermined sequences of steps and body moves choreographed to fit the specific musical structure of a particular dance. Hence, the fundamental elements of a dance consist of:

1. How we use our feet while performing sequences of steps (footwork)
2. How we allocate the beats of the music to each step we dance (timing and rhythm)
3. The movements and positions of the body while performing those steps (dance positions, and dance holds)
4. The sequences of steps that make up specific dance patterns (dance pattern building blocks)
5. The individual characteristics of each dance

The body's ability to move, its kinesthetic potential, is limitless. However, when two people need to move as one, the body's movement capabilities are somewhat limited, especially during dances when keeping body contact predominates. Most dance patterns consist of a set of sequences of steps, or blocks, that make partner dancing possible. I refer to those blocks as pattern-building blocks and include them in the group of fundamentals of dancing.

DANCE TIP:

In each of the group of lessons that follow this chapter, all fundamental components are covered in detail as they apply to the dance as well as to its main category. As the information related to these components is best acquired from text, photos, and diagrams it is only addressed in detail in the book, and addressed only in the DVD when it relates to the execution of a dance pattern.

Chapter 1

Footwork

Most dictionaries describe footwork as the manner in which feet move when dancing. In regards to social dancing, footwork is best described as the manner and direction in which areas of the feet are placed on or retrieved from the dance floor.

You might find it amazing to know that there's very little difference between how your feet move and work while you are taking a stroll down the block and how they move and work while you are dancing.

When you walk, your body and feet are in a constant interaction. They adjust their structural mechanisms according to the direction they are traveling to, the terrain they are moving on, the pace they are moving at, and even the shape of the shoes you might be wearing.

However, few people actually know that there is a correct and an incorrect way of walking. Were the learning of proper walking mechanics to be as common as learning how to tie shoelaces, many of the orthopedic lower back, hip, and knee problems afflicting three out of five Americans at least once in their lifetime would not take place. Moreover, one of the factors that determine the level of proficiency and performance between dancers, even between champion competition dancers, is how well each of them applies the mechanics of proper walking to their dancing. This is especially true in smooth dances.

The focus of this chapter is not to immerse you in a detailed study of the interaction of the one hundred bones, twenty-six muscles, and multiple joints and ligaments of the foot and how they all interact with the rest of the body every time you take a step. Yet, a certain level of familiarity with the process as it relates to social dancing is good to have for the following reason: Someone who looks stiff and robotic when they walk is likely to have an unbalanced walking fashion and is thus likely to look stiff and robotic when dancing. Conversely, someone who walks tall and with a symmetrically balanced gait is more likely to appear more relaxed and confident on the dance floor as well as more like a "natural" dancer. Which of the two would you rather look like?

Mechanics of Walking and Dancing

Let's start this interactive lesson with the mechanics of a correct walk. You won't even have to stand up. All you need to do is visualize that you are walking. Let's give it a try.

1. Take a second to visualize that at this very moment you are standing in a large, empty room. Your feet are placed next to each other about six inches apart, but your body weight is resting on your right foot. Easy to imagine, right?

2. Now, take another second or two and see yourself taking one step forward with your left foot. Ok? Now, let me ask you to visualize you taking that step again. But this time, I want you to focus on your entire body, head to toe. Done? Now, let me ask you a question, "What area of your body did you see moving first? Your left foot? Your left leg?"

If you answered, "My left foot" the information that follows will be of extreme benefit to you. The same applies if you answered, "My left leg." But if you answered, "I think the entire body moved first," you're going to be such a good dancer in such a short period you're going to amaze every one of your friends.

While the command "to walk" starts inside your head, the action of walking starts with the body's center core. This is the area that includes your abdominal and lower back muscles. The body's core is where the body's imaginary center of gravity resides. When you are about to step in any direction, the muscles within your core are immediately engaged in order for you to maintain balance. The stronger your core muscles are, the more poised you look. If you've watched professional ballroom dancers on TV, I am sure you've noticed how lean and strong their core looks.

Here's a brief explanation of the relationship between your feet and your body during two forward steps:

1. From somewhere in your brain the command "to move" is issued.

2. In fractions of a second, whichever foot you are not standing on reacts to that command and starts to move forward.

3. Halfway through the traveling foot's forward motion, the toes and ball of your weight-supporting foot starts to press down against the floor. This "push-off" action is what ultimately propels your entire body forward and onto the traveling foot. The stronger the push-off, the longer the stride of the traveling foot will be. But even in a regular size forward walk or individual forward dance step, some degree of push-off action does occur.

4. It is at the exact heel-floor-striking point that the body mechanics thus far involved in this process simulate what takes place when a plane is about to land on a runway: The rear tires (the heel of your traveling foot) touch down; the nose of the plane (the toes of the traveling foot) is up; then, as the nose of the plane lowers, its front tire (the toes and ball of the traveling foot) touches down; finally, the plane's landing gears (your knees) cushion the full impact of the weight of the plane's fuselage (your body) by spreading its full weight over all tires (your now new supporting foot).

5. Were you to take another forward step, the entire process is repeated. During a regular walking step, the seamless and smooth transition of our body's weight from one forward or backward step onto the next step and the one after constitutes one of the basic elements of correct walking mechanics. Likewise, in dance, it represents one of the fundamental elements of correct footwork mechanics found in smooth dances.

Take a look at the following photographs. They show the different phases of footwork as each relates to the body's weight shifting action.

The dance patterns of most smooth dances consist of forward and back steps which alternate between side steps. While there's a certain degree of push-off action that takes place between supporting foot and traveling foot, it is nowhere as strongly defined as it is between forward and back walks. On most side steps, it is the inside edge of the traveling foot that first strikes the floor. Likewise, it is from the inside edge of the supporting foot that a slight push-off action takes place.

Praise Those Knees

As I already mentioned our knees are our shock absorbers. If our mode of walking is not symmetrically well balanced, one or more of those two wonderful shock absorbers will eventually react in one way or the other. And reactions are not often positive ones.

Particularly in the smooth dances, the knees always end up moving in a straight line across the length of the feet. A proper ball-of-the-foot "push off" action in smooth dances is not possible when the body stands on locked knees.

In rhythm dances the knees play an even larger role in the mechanics of footwork, for it is the inter-

In this photo the dancer is starting with both feet placed together, but with his weight on the right foot. See the dotted line that runs vertically down the center of him and that ends between the heel and the ball of his foot? It is there to indicate the imaginary vertical force of gravity that travels down through the body's core and its center of balance, ending just a little ahead of the midpoint of the length of the foot.

In this photo, the body has already received the command to move forward. Look at the position of the body in relation to the dotted line. It is ahead of it, right? Also, look at the traveling foot. It has already started to move forward with a heel lead.

In this photo, the heel of the dancer's traveling foot has reached its destination. The dancer's body is standing at mid-stride. Look at the dancer's back foot. See how its heel is off the floor? It is in that position because of the push-off action being exerted by the toes and ball of the foot.

In this photo, the dancer has completed the step. Is there any difference between this photo and the first photo? No. The dancer is back at his previous starting point.

active coordination between the hips, the knees, the ankles and feet that give Latin dances that sexy Afro-Cuban characteristic style.

Learning how to walk correctly is easy. Applying correct walking mechanics is not something that happens overnight. However, the benefits of working toward that goal are felt almost instantly:

A view of the position of the traveling foot as it takes a side step.

Your ankle and calf muscles will strengthen. The everyday stress we place on knee and hip joints will lessen. You'll look and feel taller. You'll be able to walk longer distances without tiring. Your core muscles—those of the abdomen and back—will be engaged 24/7 so that you'll end up trimming inches off your waist without ever having to do a single sit-up.

Smooth Dance Footwork

Most of the dance patterns of smooth dances consist of long forward and back strides combined with short side steps. In less than a handful of exceptions, forward-moving steps are always taken with a heel lead just like in a regular walking step. Backward-moving steps are always taken with a toe/ball lead. And side steps are generally taken with the inside edge of the foot.

As I've already pointed out, when teaching dance students how to perform a correct forward or back walk some instructors will use the term "rolling" to describe how the body's weight shifts from a heel or ball of the foot lead onto the center of the moving foot.

Needless to say, it is a little more difficult for women than it is for men to push off from their supporting foot and then to shift their body's weight by "rolling" it onto the traveling foot, especially when they're moving backwards. The degree of difficulty largely depends on the style of the shoes she wears to dance in. Shoes with very high heels make proper footwork and smooth shifts in body weight more difficult as do sandals that do not have a good ankle strap. This is the reason why some ladies who like to dance will bring with them to a party an extra pair of shoes they prefer to wear when the party goes from a ceremonial phase, as in weddings, to a full-out party and dancing phase after the cake is cut. Doing so will not only help you dance all night, it will also avoid the much-too-often "these shoes are killing me" syndrome.

It is both the strength and the flexibility of our own ankles and feet that allow us to gradually roll the body's weight from the heel to the center of the foot and then onto the ball and toes. If the physiological structure of the feet and ankles didn't facilitate the various ways by which they can move and flex, the way we walked would look more like a military march—placing our body weight in one single, downward, stomp—or very similar to how four-legged animals walk.

Look at the following three photos to see what transpires when we break down a forward and a backward step musical count by musical count.

On the first count of the two-count slow (S) move, the body is balanced between the front heel of the left foot and the back toe of the right foot.

As the second step is taken, notice how the heel of the supporting foot (LF) has risen and how the traveling foot (RF) has already started to move ahead.

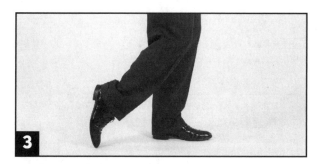

On the second count of the two-count slow (S) move, the weight has been fully transferred onto the front half of the first moving foot (LF).

Conversely, it is from the inside edge of the supporting foot that a push-off action takes place prior to the taking of a side step. However, a sideward push-off action is never as strong because the distance between side steps is that much shorter than the distance between forward and backward moving steps.

There is another reason why the characteristic footwork of smooth dances is a heel lead on forward moving steps, a toe-ball lead on backward moving steps, and a whole-foot weight placement on side steps. That reason is rhythm.

With the exception of the waltz, forward and backward steps in the two other smooth dances, the foxtrot and the tango, generally take two counts to complete. Side steps take only one count to complete.

Latin and Rhythm Footwork

It is easy to single out a good Latin or swing dancer from a crowd of dancers. The manner in which isolated movements of the shoulders, the arms, the rib cage, the hips and feet all come together is an exciting thing to watch. Much of it comes down to footwork. In rhythm dances the mechanics of footwork are totally different from the mechanics of smooth dances.

First, forward and back steps are taken with the ball of the feet, not with the heels.

Second, the body's weight is placed or pressed down into the whole foot instead of being rolled onto the foot.

Third, there's no push-off action from the supporting foot to the moving foot. Instead, the ultimate shift of weight takes place because the upper body has continued to move forward. The body's entire weight is now resting on the entire foot.

STAIR-CLIMBING VISUAL EXERCISE

Let me give you another visual aid exercise to explain the process of a rhythm walk, especially as it applies to Latin dances and, in some ways, also to dances like the Swing and the Hustle.

1. Visualize yourself going up a flight of stairs, starting with your left foot? Ok? Question: *Did you take that step by first placing your heel on the step, the ball of the foot, or the entire foot?*

The correct answer is: "I stepped on the ball of the foot, then my weight went onto the flat foot as I climbed the step."

How did you do?

2. Let's climb that same step with the left foot. But before you do, I want you to focus on two things: (1) The hip of the weight-bearing leg, and (2) the knee above the foot that you use to take the step. Ok? Go!

Question 1: "*As you took that second step, what did the hip of your weight-bearing leg, your right leg, do?*"

The correct answer is, *"It shifted further over to the right."*

Question 2: "*What was the position of the left knee in relation to the left foot?*"

The correct answer is, *"The knee was bent right over the toes of the left foot."*

Two-part question: "*As you were moving your body from the weight-supporting right leg over to the stair-climbing left foot, (1) what was the position of your body in relation to the left leg, and (2) what did the left knee do when it absorbed the impact of the body's weight as you completed the step?*"

The correct answer to 1 is, *"From my waist up my body was leaning over the left knee."*

The correct answer to 2 is, *"As my body continued to lean forward, the left knee started to straighten."*

Congratulations! You've just performed all the mechanics of weight transference and of footwork involved in rhythm dances.

Chapter 2

Timing and Rhythm

You have rhythm. Yes. You do. Lots of it!

We're born with an already developing sense of rhythm. As we mature, some of us express it through music we enjoy listening to, lyrics we sing, or by learning to play an instrument. Others express it through physical activities like dancing, sports and athletics. But even those who are not musically, physically or athletically inclined possess a sense of rhythm they may not be aware they have, but will recognize in others.

When someone tells me, "I have no rhythm," I respond with, "When was the last time you heard yourself talking? How you space the words within a sentence or phrase that you say, how you accent some and hush others, how you link some words and enunciate others. What do you think that is? Where do you think it all comes from?"

It's rhythm and it comes from within!

Of course, when it comes to social dancing there is a very important reason why your sense of rhythm needs to be developed and channeled in a couple of ways. Any clues why?

Ever heard the phrase, "It takes two to tango?"

That's right. Dance patterns follow a rhythmic structure. When you dance, you and your partner need to link your own senses of rhythm to the pattern's own rhythm.

Good social dancers are those who can blend how they feel the music during the performance of a dance step into one rhythmic structure without losing their own individual sense of rhythm. A mouthful, I know. But that's just the way it is. And the easiest and fastest way to figure out how to do that is by first learning the basic structure of dance music.

So, let's start with our lesson. Let your feet rest and get your fingers ready. All I want you to do is pop the DVD into the player, read the instructions that follow, then use your remote to click on the DVD chapter titled Timing and Rhythm.

Timing

Dance music is always composed along the lines of a mathematical formula that follows a sequential order: "Beats" (Counts) are grouped into "Measures" (Bars) which are grouped into "Phrases" which are grouped into "Choruses" that generally repeat themselves any number of times,

A beat of music is an audibly defined single sound made by either one or a group of musical instruments. A beat is the basic unit of any orchestral composition.

BASIC MUSIC STRUCTURE OF DANCE MUSIC

Beats/Counts Sequences

12345678   12345678   12345678   12345678

Down Beats within a Beat/Count Sequence

1<u>2</u>3<u>4</u>5<u>6</u>7<u>8</u>   1<u>2</u>3<u>4</u>5<u>6</u>7<u>8</u>   1<u>2</u>3<u>4</u>5<u>6</u>7<u>8</u>   1<u>2</u>3<u>4</u>5<u>6</u>7<u>8</u>

Up Beats within a Beat/Count Sequence

1<u>2</u>3<u>4</u>5<u>6</u>7<u>8</u>   1<u>2</u>3<u>4</u>5<u>6</u>7<u>8</u>   1<u>2</u>3<u>4</u>5<u>6</u>7<u>8</u>   1<u>2</u>3<u>4</u>5<u>6</u>7<u>8</u>

Beats/Counts Grouped in a Musical Measure

<u>1234</u>   <u>5678</u>   <u>1234</u>   <u>5678</u>   <u>1234</u>   <u>5678</u>   <u>1234</u>   <u>5678</u> = 8 Measures

Beats/Counts Grouped in a Musical Phrase

8 Measures 8 Measures 8 Measures 8 Measures = 1 Phrase

A measure generally consists of a group of four beats (4/4), except in the waltz which consists of only three (3/4). However, there are dance arrangements in which a measure may consist of a group of two counts (2/4) and even 6/4. But few of the dances performed to that musical structure are included in this book.

In each measure of music there are two accented beats: the first and third beats. The first beat, the "one" beat is the most accented of the four. Both the first and the third beat are each called "down beats." The second and fourth beat are each called "up beats."

A dance pattern consists of a sequence of "steps." All dances have at least one signature dance pattern. Some have two plus variations of each. Subsequently, the pattern of any dance, from its basic to its most advanced, is structured according to an even distribution of musical beats and measures. Generally, there are two to four measures per dance pattern.

This structure is deliberately choreographed in a manner that, generally, calls for dancers to start the first step of a dance pattern on the "one" beat and to complete that pattern on an upbeat, usually either the fourth or eight beat, depending on the amount of individual steps and beats found within a dance pattern. Learning how to audibly distinguish the difference between down and up beats is essential to a dancer dancing "on time" to the music.

Rhythm

In social dance, rhythm refers to the number of beats that it takes to complete one individual step within a dance pattern. One beat per step makes that step a quick step (Q). Two beats per step makes that step a slow step (S). There can be several combinations of slow and quick steps within one dance pattern, but the most common ones are: Slow Quick Quick (SQQ), and Slow Slow Quick Quick (SSQQ).

BASIC RHYTHMS OF DANCE PATTERNS

Beats/Counts in Rhythmic Groups

Slow Quick Quick (SQQ):

<u>1</u> 2 3 4 <u>5</u> 6 7 8   <u>1</u> 2 3 4 <u>5</u> 6 7 8
S   Q Q S   Q Q   S   Q Q S   Q Q

Quick Quick Slow (QQS):

1 2 <u>3</u> 4 5 <u>6 7 8</u>   1 2 <u>3</u> 4 5 <u>6 7 8</u>
Q Q S   Q Q S   Q Q S   Q Q S

Slow Slow Quick Quick (SSQQ):

<u>1</u> 2 <u>3</u> 4 <u>5 6</u>   <u>7</u> 8 <u>1</u> 2 <u>3 4</u>   <u>5</u> 6 <u>7</u> 8 <u>1 2</u>   <u>3</u> 4 <u>5</u> 6 <u>7 8</u>
S   S   Q Q   S   S   Q Q   S   S   Q Q   S   S   Q Q

The combination of Slow and Quick rhythm is more characteristic of smooth dances than it is of Rhythm and Latin dances where we count individual beats per step. In both dance styles, the most common distribution of beats per step is 1 to 1. Exceptions to that rule are the waltz, which is always counted 1, 2, 3 and the rumba which can be counted in beats 1, 2, 3, 4 or in QQS and also SQQ, the basic rhythm of the slower tempo rumba (bolero).

Helping you distinguish the "down" and "up beats" of a measure of music, and how to then group them into "quick" and "slow" steps is the focus of this lesson. So get your ears tuned up and don't be frustrated if you can't hear the differences right away. Just as it takes practice to perfect dance patterns, musical training doesn't happen over night.

DVD LESSON:

It's time to click "Play" on the *Let's Dance* DVD. From your MENU page, select TIMING & RHYTHM. But before you click "Play" again, let me tell you what you're going to see and hear.

This is a musical appreciation lesson. It lasts about two minutes. It is divided into five segments, each about 20 seconds long. The objective of each progressive segment is to help you identify individual beats, down and up beats, slow beats and combinations of slow and quick beats. This is how each segment works.

1. First, you're going to hear a couple of measures of a musical tune.
2. Then, you're going to see a special-effects graphic appearing onscreen and hear my voice counting each beat. Count along with me.
3. All of a sudden, I will stop counting. But you are to continuing listening to the music, tapping your fingers to the beat or counting out loud.
4. See if your finger tapping still matches the graphic's pulse. If it doesn't, you know you have to listen more keenly.

The song will play for 30 seconds and fade into the "Down and Up Beats." In that same manner, you will continue to listen to the song, tapping your fingers all the way through the last segment: Slow and Quick Rhythms.

Chapter 3

Dance Stance, Frames, Positions, and Holds

Social dances fall into three categories: smooth, Latin, and rhythm. Each category features its own characteristic dance stance, dance frame, dance positions and dance holds.

Dance stance relates to the body posture maintained by dancers. Dance frame relates to the position of the dancers' arms in relation to one another. Dance position relates to the positions of the dancer's bodies within the performance of a sequence of individual steps. Dance hold refers to the manner in which dancers maintain contact with each other within the performance of a sequence of individual steps.

Dance Stances, Frames, Positions and Holds in Smooth Dances

THE SMOOTH DANCER'S STANCE

How a dance couple stands in relation to each other is referred to as their dance stance. This calls for dance partners to stand tall, holding their shoulders down and with their body weight firmly placed toward the front of their feet. Knees are kept at a relaxed angle. They are never to be in a locked position.

Dancers in smooth dance stance.

The Smooth Dancer's Frame

How partners hold each other while dancing is referred to as their dance frame. The characteristic, universally standardized, correct dance frame for smooth ballroom dances—waltz, foxtrot, and tango—calls for dancers to maintain body contact and for their bodies and arms to be placed as follows:

1. Ladies stand off to the right side of their partners, maintaining a left leaning curve that starts at the base of the lower spine and ends at the top of the head. Ladies' heads are to have a slight tilt to the left, looking over men's right shoulder. Men's bodies stand tall with a firm core and shoulders down.

2. The arms of both partners are kept up and to the sides at about chest level with their elbows in a bent position. Were a line to be drawn connecting partners' elbow, it would run horizontally to the dance floor and across the shoulder blades of both partners.

3. The ladies' left forearm is to rest over the men's right upper arm, without pressing down on it. The heel of a lady's left hand is to rests just below the seam of a man's right jacket sleeve. Her fingers stay close and rest over the seam of the sleeve.

4. The man places the heel of his right hand just below the woman's left shoulder blade, without pressing into her back. (A very important point, as well). His fingers stay closed together. Nothing is uglier than the open hand of a man, especially a groom, over the beautiful gown of his partner or bride.

The palm of the man's left hand and the palm of the woman's right hand are joined together in a firm clasp with the fingers overlapping each other's hand.

especially when dancing with someone they don't know very well, and therefore fear they might step on their partner's feet. For those reasons many dance instructors start their beginner students with a more relaxed dance frame often referred to as "the social dance frame" that doesn't call for body contact.

1. In a social dance frame, arms are not necessarily held at chest level and can be held further down both sides of the body. In this case, the imaginary horizontal line that connects left and right elbows runs under the shoulder blades and not across the dancers' center.

2. The position of the dancers' arms and the clasp of their hands remain the same as for the standard ballroom dance frame.

Smooth Dance Positions

Closed Dance Position Hold (CL)

The Closed Dance Position (CL) is the characteristic dance position of the smooth dances. Beginners do not need to maintain body contact in CL dance position. However, more experienced dancers are generally expected to. Most other dance positions take their name according to the direction in which a man leads his partner, for example Left Open

Social Dance Frame

When first learning how to dance, some people will find the standard ballroom dance frame a bit too formal. Others are intimidated by the close body contact,

Dancers in a more relaxed social dance frame.

DANCE TIP:

Maintaining the proper stance and dance frame during dancing is very important. Were the woman not to stand off to the right of her partner, the man's forward view would be obstructed by her head. He needs a clear view of what lies ahead all the time so as not to bump into other couples.

Maintaining this parallel foot placement is what will keep partners from stepping on each other's toes while dancing in close dance position.

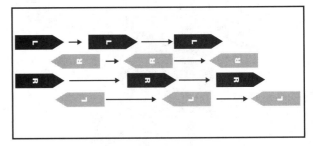

Footprint diagram of feet in their four lanes of traffic.

Position (LO), or according to the position she's placed in relation to his own position, such as Right or Left Side Position. Sometimes, partners will change dance positions two or three times within an individual dance pattern.

Another important element while in a Closed Dance Position is the actual position of partners' feet in relation to each other. By the woman standing off to the right of her partner, rather than facing him squarely, she's adding two extra, parallel, lanes of foot traffic. Meaning, her right foot moves on a parallel lane located between two other parallel lanes, one for the man's left foot and the other for his right foot. Her left foot then runs along a fourth parallel lane located just outside of the man's right foot lane.

Left Open Dance Position (LO)

It is called the Left Open Dance Position (LO) because as he takes a step the man opens the left side of his body away from his partner's right side. The woman follows the lead by opening the right side of her body away from the left side of her partner. In the Left Open Dance Position both partners then step forward facing the same direction. The Left Open Dance Position hold is often called the "promenade" position. All the smooth dance patterns featured in this book are danced in either the Closed Dance Position, the Left Open Dance Position, or in an alternating combination of both.

Partners moving in LO dance position.

Dance Stance, Frame, Positions and Holds in Latin and Rhythm Dances

While dancing Latin and rhythm dances, partners maintain a forward-leaning posture.

This stance places more of the body's weight over the front of the thighs and the balls of the feet. It also allows for better flexing and straightening of the knees and for the side-to-side hip action, the Cuban motion, that characterizes Latin dances.

THE LATIN DANCER'S FRAME

The dance frame for Latin and rhythm dances is much more relaxed than the dance frame for smooth dances in order to facilitate the various changes of dance positions and dance holds that can take place within one dance pattern. Elbows are held farther down along the sides of the body. The man's right hand is also placed lower down the back of his partner's spine. As you will see in our DVD, most of the patterns in dances like the salsa/mambo and the cha-cha can actually be danced with partners holding each other in a variety of ways.

LATIN AND RHYTHM DANCE POSITIONS

In Latin and rhythm dances there are a myriad of dance positions. The names of some are directly related to how partners stay in contact ("Dance Hold") during a dance pattern. Others are named according to the positions of their bodies in relation to one another. For beginners, the variety of holds

Dance stance for Latin and rhythm dance.

and positions can be daunting. Fortunately, at a social level, there are only a couple of dance positions to become familiar with.

Closed Dance Position (CL)

In Closed Dance Position (CL), dancers face each other maintaining a Latin dance frame.

Dance frame during Latin and rhythm dances.

Dancers in Latin CL Dance Position.

Open Dance Positions (O)

In Open Dance Positions, dancers break away from their standard dance frame, but will stay in contact through either a One-Hand Hold (1HH) or a Two-Hand Hold (2HH). Our dance patterns feature two Open Dance Positions—the Left Open and the Right Open—both of which can be danced in a Closed Dance Position Frame or in a One- or Two-Hand Hold.

Partners facing each other in a One-Hand Hold (1HH) Open Position.

Partners facing each other in a Two-Hand Hold (2HH) Open Position.

Partners moving in a Left Open Position with a 1HH.

Partners moving in a Right Open Position with a 1HH.

Apart Dance Position (A)

In this position, partners have no contact and stand either facing each other, next to each other (side-by-side) or with one partner facing the back of the other partner ("Shine Position"). Most turns and spins are danced in Apart Dance Position (A).

Partners in Apart Dance Position, facing each other.

Partners in Apart Dance Position, standing side-by-side.

LATIN DANCER'S HOLDS

In most of the Open Dance Positions, partners clasp their hands differently than they do in Closed Dance Position: The palms of the man's hands face upward. The palms of the woman's hands face downward and are placed on the palms of the man's hands. This clasp is referred to as "palm-to-palm."

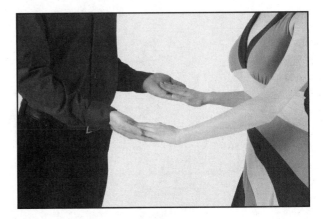

Palm-to-palm clasp in Two-Hand Hold.

Chapter 4

Dance Pattern Building Blocks

When two dancers are moving as one, the range of their legs' motion and the directions they can travel in are generally limited to forward, backward, and side. Were it any other way, leading and following a dance pattern would be difficult if not impossible. Fortunately, this limitation works in the dancers' favor in a myriad of ways, one of them being the learning of dance patterns.

Social dance patterns consist of sequences of individual steps which move in one of those three directions, or that move in a combination of two or three directions—forward and side-ways, sideways and back, and so on. By grouping these combinations, we arrive at four specific walking-movement patterns. All dance patterns, especially at a social/beginner level, consist of combinations of these four groups. I call these four groups the Dance Pattern Building Blocks. They are:

1. A Forward and Back Walk
2. A Side-to-Side Walk
3. A Forward, Back and Side-to-Side Rock/Breaks
4. A Box Step

FOOTPRINTS, PHOTOS AND THE MIRROR OPPOSITE FACTOR

In the social-level signature patterns of most dances the woman's foot placements, are generally the exact opposites of her partner's—the mirror opposite. However, that is not always the case during turns and spins, most of which are led by the man and performed by the woman.

The Forward and Back Walks

In the smooth dances, most dance patterns call for one to two consecutive forward or back walks. The tango's basic step is an exception, with three consecutive forward walks (for the men) and three back walks (for the women). In the Latin and rhythm dances, most dance patterns call for just one forward or back walk. Some dance patterns include a "tap" step at the end of a forward/back walk, allowing dancers to reverse direction. A "tap" step, danced with just the toe or ball of the foot tapping the dance floor, is not considered a full step because the weight of the body is never shifted onto a tapping foot.

STEP	M—FOOT PLACEMENT	W—FOOT PLACEMENT
1	Fwd with LF	Bk with RF
2	Fwd with RF	Bk with LF
3	Fwd with LF	Bk with RF
4	Tap RF next to LF	Tap LF next to RF
5	Bk with RF	Fwd with LF
6	Bk with LF	Fwd with RF
7	Bk with RF	Fwd with LF
8	Tap LF next to RF	Tap RF next to LF

DANCE TIP (For Men):

Initiate each step with a heel lead then roll the weight of the body from the center of the foot to the base of the toes, pushing off from the toes as you take the second step. Keep your knees flexible throughout.

DANCE TIP (For Women):

Initiate each step with a toe/ball lead then roll the weight of the body from the center of the foot to the heel, pushing off from that heel as you take the second step. Whenever you shift your weight onto a forward or backward step, it is on the middle of the foot that the greatest impact of the body's weight is felt. To soften that impact, our knees need to soften, to bend slightly toward the front of the supporting foot. Moreover, it is that bending action that then allows the ankle of the supporting foot to flex, helping you push off from the toes of that supporting foot onto the next foot. The rolling action I've been speaking of can never take place smoothly on locked knees.

The Side-to-Side Walks

Side-to-side walks are frequently called a *Chassé* or a *Triple Step*. One of the most important things to be learned from a side-to-side walk is how the body's weight is shifted or changed (WC) the moment the traveling foot closes next to the supporting foot. This is one of the main rules of partner dancing: *Whenever a moving foot closes next to a supporting foot an automatic change of weight must take place with the body's weight immediately going onto the traveling foot thus freeing the supporting foot to move.* The only exception to this rule is a "tapping" step" where there's never a weight change (NWC).

Step	M & W—Foot Placement
1	Step to the Left with the LF
2	Close RF to LF (WC)
3	Step to the Left again with the LF
4	Reverse direction and step to the Right with the RF
5	Close LF to RF (WC)
6	Step to the Right again with the RF

DANCE TIP:

Most side-to-side steps are executed at a "syncopated rhythmic speed"—three steps in only two beats of music. Because the distance between steps needs to be small in order to avoid jumping or hoping from step to step, there's very little push-off action taking place from the inside edge of the feet. The feet then slide the weight sideways instead of rolling or pressing it.

The Forward and Back and Side-to-Side Rock/Breaks

A rocking move is generally done with feet placed one in front of the other or side-by-side. Most rocking moves are completed in just two single steps. In dance, we use the term "rock" to describe a movement during which the body moves forward and back, or side-to-side, shifting weight from one foot to the other. In Latin and rhythm dances, we often refer to a "rock" step as a "break" step because the second step stops the body from moving farther in one direction, allowing it to immediately reverse direction. Rock/breaks are the predominant pattern building block of the dance patterns of most Latin dances.

FORWARD AND BACK ROCK BREAKS

Step	M & W—Foot Placement
1	Step Fwd with the LF
2	Step Bk In Place (In-Pl) with RF
3	Close the LF to the RF (WC)
4	Step Bk with the RF
5	Step Fwd In-Pl with the LF
6	Close the RF to the LF (WC)

SIDE-TO-SIDE ROCK BREAKS

Step	M & W—Foot Placement
1	Step Side (Sd) with LF
2	Step Sd In-Pl with RF
3	Close LF to RF (WC)
4	Step Sd with RF
5	Step Side In-Pl with LF
6	Close RF to LF (WC)

The Box Step

The Box Step, in essence, consists of a combination of forward, back and side steps. The Box Step is the pattern building block of the signature dance pattern of the foxtrot, the waltz, and the rumba.

As you know, a square box is made up of two triangles. Thus the Box Step consists of two triangles. We refer to each triangle as "a half Box Step." There is the forward half and the back half.

The forward half is the one that always starts when a dancer steps forward on the left foot.

Step	M & W—Foot Placement
1	Fwd with LF
2	Sd with RF
3	Close LF to RF (WC)

The backward half is the one that always starts when a dancer steps backward on the right foot.

Step	M & W—Foot Placement
1	Bk with RF
2	Sd with LF
3	Close RF to LF (WC)

So, when you put the two halves together, you have a full Box Step:

Step	M & W—Foot Placement
1	Step Fwd with LF
2	Step Sd with RF
3	Close LF to RF (WC)
4	Step Bk with RF
5	Step Sd with LF
6	Close RF to LF (WC)

DANCE TIP:

Remember the rule we learned earlier: When the traveling foot closes up to the supporting foot, the body's weight automatically shifts from the supporting foot to the traveling foot, freeing that foot to take another step.

DANCE TIP:

On what foot was your body's weight at the completion of the third move? If you said on the left foot, you did the above correctly. If you said on the right foot, then you didn't shift the weight to the left foot the moment it closed next to the right foot.

DVD LESSON:

The Triple Step, the Rock Breaks and the Box Step are shown on your DVD in the Fundamentals of the Smooth and the Rhythm Dances.

Chapter 5

Individual Characteristics

Every dance has something—a body move, a combination of pattern building blocks, a rhythm—by which it is identified and distinguished from other dances.

In the smooth dances, the signature characteristics are:

- an upright body stand;
- an unwavering dance frame;
- long forward and backward strides;
- heel leads on forward steps and toe/ball leads on back steps;
- the left-curving position of a woman's torso while in Closed Dance Position;
- Balance Steps and Box Steps; and
- the distribution of musical counts into Slow and Quick counts.

There are also a number of characteristics that are unique to each smooth dance even in cases where they share the same dance pattern.

For example, the Box Step is choreographically the same for the foxtrot, the waltz, and the rumba. But in the foxtrot, the Box Step is danced with a gliding foot action. In the waltz, the Box Step is danced with a rise-and-fall of the feet and with the body leaning (swaying) to the left or to the right between side steps. In the rumba, the Box Step starts with a side step instead of a forward or back step.

In addition, there are many standard styling characteristics that become the foundation upon which dancers develop many of their own arm and body movements. In the Latin dances, for examples, women have the freedom to move their free arm in a variety of ways often giving the simplest patterns a very showy look. In some of the Latin dances featured on our DVD my dance partners will show our female readers a number of simple arm and hand styling movements they can add to dance patterns like underarm turns, cross over and walk around turns, etc.

Part Two

The Smooth Dances

The waltz, the foxtrot, and the tango make up the smooth dance category of *Let's Dance*. These three dances share many of the same fundamental elements, but each dance also has unique characteristics of its own.

The waltz, the oldest of the three, is known for its grace and poise. Its 3/4 rhythm, where the "one" count is followed by two highly accented "up beat" counts, lends itself to the dance's characteristic body swaying and knee bending-and-straightening dance pattern. For centuries, waltzes have been considered a "formal" dance, played at the balls of kings and queens, and as the "opening" dance of social events like weddings and debutante balls.

The foxtrot is often referred to as the dance of inaugural balls and wedding receptions. Many credit an American vaudevillian, Harry Fox, as the originator of the foxtrot because he performed a dance later coined "the fox" at a New York City Ziegfield Follies review in 1913. However, it was a couple of famous dancers of that era, Vernon and Irene Castle, who are credited for making the foxtrot into a partner dance.

In their traditional, standardized, choreographic format foxtrot dance patterns move in a counter-clock direction on the dance floor referred to as the "line of dance." There are two predominant foxtrot dance styles: the American style and the International style. Each style features different levels of proficiency. Many foxtrot patterns crisscross the floor in gliding turns that often lead dancers into beautifully posed movements.

Unquestionably, the tango is the most daring of the three smooth dances. In Argentina, it was a popular dance among its poorest classes but given the cold shoulder by its high society. Then, in the 1920s, wealthy Argentinians, who had gone to study in Paris, popularized the dance. There are various styles of tango: the Argentine tango, the English or International style tango, and the American tango. All three share a closed dance position as their characteristic dance position, although in the Argentine tango couples hold each other in an even tighter embrace. They also share many picture-posing moves like lunges, oversways, flicks and fans.

Chapter 6

The Waltz

The waltz originates from the German word "waltzen," which means to turn, roll or glide. Origins of the waltz date as far back as the early seventeenth century when Austrian peasants performed the Weller, a folk dance characterized by robust and rigid movements. Adaptations of the Weller were then incorporated into the Allemande and the Minuet, two court dances favored by the French aristocracy during the mid-eighteenth century.

During the latter part of the eighteenth century another Austrian folk dance emerged. It was called the Landler. But it was not until the early nineteenth century that young men chose to dance the Landler by placing their right hand around a woman's waist, bringing dance couples in closer body contact than ever before. It was a bold move that was immediately condemned by religious leaders who thought of it as being obscene, wicked, contagiously amoral. As a result, the Landler waltz soon became known as "the forbidden dance."

During the mid-1800s, three great Austrian composers, Franz Lanner, Johann Straus, Sr., and Johann Straus, Jr., paved the way for a final acceptance of a closer dance hold. Their version of the waltz, the Viennese Waltz, boasted a faster tempo that made it difficult for dancers to perform this style of waltz's more compact left and right turns unless they held their bodies in closer contact and their arms in a locked and more equally balanced "frame." It was then that the formerly controversial close dance position became progressively popular and more accepted in social circles, especially when it was rumored that Queen Victoria herself loved the Viennese Waltz.

Around the time of the First World War, a new form of the waltz started to flourish in the city of Boston under the name of "The Boston." The waltz's traditional 3/4 rhythm was played at a slower tempo (136-144 beats per minute), and the turning patterns were not as sharp as those of the Viennese Waltz. Whereas dancers still had to maintain a firm hold or "dance frame" and close body contact, the turns of the now-called "modern waltz" could be achieved with longer forward and sideward strides of three to six foot movements.

The Boston's popularity was short-lived. Many years later, in England, the waltz resurfaced thanks to the work of that country's top dance masters who set out to revise the dance's basic elements. Their work resulted in a series of well-thought-of techniques which combined challenging body mechanics with very precise descriptions on foot placement, on footwork and on the degree of turning range allowed for each individual step. Ultimately, their work became the pedestal upon which other techniques were developed, all giving rise to a universally standardized and accepted waltz style known by names like "the modern waltz," "the English waltz" or the "International waltz."

As elegant and simple as any style of waltz can look, it is a dance professional dance competitors spend endless hours practicing. Some beginner dance students find the quick shift of weight, that takes place on the three count when feet come together, difficult to master at first. But, practice is the key as is often the case with all new steps and dance levels. One thing is for certain: when you can waltz adoring eyes will follow you wherever you go.

I've chosen to start Part Two of this book with the waltz for one reason. The study of the waltz's fundamental dance elements and patterns provide a wonderful foundation that will help you when you

---

THE WEDDING AND PARTY WALTZ

That a dance once labeled as scandalous, vulgar and sinful ultimately evolved into the twentieth century's official wedding dance has been a feat not experienced by any other dance.

Over the years, there have been many waltz compositions and lyrics that have become favored father-daughter wedding dances. Some have been around for a long time: "Fascination," "Moon River," "The Tennessee Waltz." Others are more contemporary: "You Light Up My Life," "Could I Have This Dance," "Sunrise Sunset." But all are slow tempo waltzes that lend themselves to dancing a few simple and easy-to-learn patterns like the ones you'll find in this book's waltz's chapter.

---

learn the foxtrot and the tango, the two dances that follow in Part Two of this book.

Fundamental Elements of the Waltz

FOOTWORK (FT)

There was a time when the waltz was danced with people sliding on their feet and rising on their toes, even on their tiptoes. Today, the correct waltz footwork calls for dancers to take all forward steps on the heel of the foot, all back steps on the ball of the foot, and most side steps either on the ball of the foot or on the inside edge of the moving foot.

"Rise and Fall," a dance term that indicates an elevation of the body by rising up on one's feet and then coming back down onto the whole foot, is one of the waltz's unique footwork characteristic elements. But when first learning how to waltz it is best for beginners not to have to worry about this fundamental element, but to instead perform the characteristic down-and-up look of a waltz solely by the action of the knees and the ankles—a "no foot rise."

No-Foot-Rise Footwork

To better understand what no foot rise is all about, let's take a look at one of the waltz's signature dance patterns—the forward and back balance steps. It consists of just one single forward step on count 1, keeping the body from moving on counts 2 and 3, then one single backward step on count 4 also keeping the body from moving on counts 5 and 6.

On count 1, as the body's weight is transferred to either the forward or backward stepping foot, the knee softens the impact of the body's weight much like the spring coils of a mattress do when one sits or lies on it. This spring-like action and how it relates to rise and fall movement, holds true for both men and women.

On count 2, as a second step is about to be taken, the knee then starts to spring back up into a normal dance stance.

On count 1, the knees are in a slightly bent angle.

On count 2, the body starts to rise as the knee starts to straighten.

STEP	COUNT	M—FOOT PLACEMENT	W—FOOT PLACEMENT
1	1	Step Fwd with LF	Step Bk with RF
2	2	Hold the position	Hold the position
3	3	Hold the position	Hold the position
4	4	Step Bk with RF	Step Fwd with LF
5	5	Hold the position	Hold the position
6	6	Hold the position	Hold the position

On count 3, as the third step is taken, the knee comes to its fully extended, although never locked, dance stance position.

On count 4, as the first step of the second musical measure is taken, the supporting knee is at its most flexed position. The traveling foot has already reached the position for its next step.

On counts 5 and 6, the body gradually resumes the proper dance stance.

On count 3, the body is back to its upright dance position during the first half of count 3, but the knee is never in a locked position. On the second half of count 3, the knee then starts to soften again as a new step (on count 4) is about to be taken.

The backward half of a balance step has commenced. Notice how the knee of the supporting foot is flexed, while the knee of the traveling foot is extended.

TIMING AND RHYTHM (T & R)

Three beats to a measure of music (3/4), with the heaviest accent being on the first beat, is the waltz's timing. Because partners step on every single beat, the dance's rhythm is equal to its timing structure.

DANCE STANCE, FRAMES, POSITIONS, AND HOLDS

As with all three smooth dances, waltz dancers are expected to keep their bodies standing tall—the dance stance. The vast majority of waltz dance patterns, including intermediate and advance patterns, are performed in Closed Dance Position (CL). The knees are never locked and the shoulders should be kept down, regardless of their having to support a wide dance frame.

In a Closed Dance Position, the man places his partner off to his right. The right side of the woman's body is placed off to the right of an imaginary vertical line that runs down the center of his body. Her upper body maintains a left-leaning curve that starts at her lower spine and ends at the crown of the head. Her neck must show an elongated,

graceful line, and her head will have a slight tilt to the left. Her correct dance stance will allow her partner to have a clear frontal view of other couples on the dance floor.

Another important element while in a Closed Dance Position is the actual position of partners' feet in relation to each other. Remember that the woman should stand off to the right of her partner, rather than facing him squarely, so that her feet are located in parallel lanes with his feet. Maintaining this parallel foot placement is what will keep partners from stepping on each other's toes while dancing in closed dance position.

Characteristic dance frame for smooth dances.

Maintaining a clear view over the woman's shoulder is important for the man.

The position of dance partner's arms is referred to as the "dance frame." The elbows are held out and to the sides of the body, as if resting on an imaginary horizontal line that runs across the middle of a dancer's shoulder blades, connecting the elbows. Keeping the arms in the correct frame position does take time and practice.

The man's left forearm is held up from its elbow at a 90-degree angle. The left hand and wrist are held firmly and in direct line with the forearm.

The heel or the man's right hand is placed on the woman's back, just under her left shoulder blade, and with fingers closed and stacked on top of each other. Men do not lead with the fingers of the right hand.

The man's dance frame.

They lead with the entire hand, moving it slightly from its wrist as if it were a hinge.

While the man's arms are placed under the woman's arms, the woman is never to think of them as a place of rest. She must hold her own. The role of the man's dance frame is to guide his partner on the dance floor but not to carry his partner on it.

Her left forearm is placed over the man's right upper arm. Her left wrist is generally placed just under the seam of the man's right jacket sleeve, and her fingers should be kept close together and cupping the man's right shoulder.

The palm of her right hand is placed against the palm of her partner's left hand with fingers draping over the outer edge of his index finger in a soft clasp.

The woman's dance frame.

DANCE PATTERN BUILDING BLOCKS

The pattern building blocks of the waltz are the forward and back walks, and the side-to-side walks. Both patterns include a "tap step" which immediately follows the full transfer of weight from the supporting foot to the traveling foot. The combination of a single forward, back or side step that is followed by a tap step is referred to as a "balance step" or a "hesitation step."

A Tap Step

While a tap is a movement that involves the foot, a tap step is not in itself considered "a step" because the body's weight is never transferred over to it. In the waltz, and even in the foxtrot, a tap step comes in handy because it helps you keep correct timing as you're holding musical counts without shifting weight. However, one must also be aware that when you are first learning how to waltz there'll be a tendency to tap and then transfer weight onto the tapping step; doing this will not allow you to re-step on that foot, something you'll have to do.

The Square Box Pattern Building Block

A tap step.

The lead into most waltz patterns is the square box step. It consists of a total of six individual steps divided into two groups each consisting of three individual steps. Some teachers, myself included, refer to each of the two groups as "the forward half of a box step" and "the back half of a box step." The

foot placements for man a and a woman in a box step are the mirror opposites of each other.

There are many reasons why a box step should be the dance pattern you should practice most. One of those reasons is to get you used to the two changes of direction that take place within two individual steps—a forward or back step immediately followed by a side step. The other reason is to teach you the application of one of the most important rules in partner dancing: *whenever a traveling foot is moving sideways to either the left or the right, aiming to end up, or closing, right next to a supporting foot, the body's weight shifts from the supporting foot to the traveling foot the moment the traveling foot hits its mark.*

In this book, we refer to all shifts taking place from one supporting foot to one traveling foot by the abbreviation "WC" (for "weight change"). Sometimes, as is the case during tap steps, a traveling foot will close up to the supporting foot but a shift of weight is not to take place. In these cases, we specify that no shift of weight takes place with the abbreviations "NWC" (or "no weight change").

Step	M & W—Foot Placement
1	Fwd with LF
2	Sd with RF
3	Close LF to RF (WC)
4	Bk with RF
5	Sd with LF
6	Close RF to LF (WC)

CHARACTERISTIC STYLES OF THE WALTZ

Body Sway

The characteristic movement of the waltz simulates the down-up-up-down-up-up motion of a pendulum. When moving forward or back the pendulum motion is a slight one. When moving side to side it is a little more obvious. Side-to-side pendulum action is referred to as the Waltz's Sway.

Basically, body sway consists of a sideways motion that starts as one hip swings in the direction of the side step being taken, causing the upper body to lean in the opposite direction. For example, if you were stepping to the side with your right foot your upper body would sway to the left. New dance students tend to approach a sway by bending from the waist. This is incorrect. Even during a swaying movement the upper torso must maintain an upright position.

The Side-to-Side Balance is the perfect pattern in which to learn about body sway. A sway is a movement that mostly involves the upper part of the body. It consists of a left or right leaning action in opposition to the moving foot. So if we're taking a side step to the left, the upper body leans to the right. In more advance movements, i.e. closed box turning moves, body sway involves the feet, the hip and the upper body.

Body sway is never to look as obvious as the ferns of a palm tree fighting a gale force wind. It is to be a gentle movement that adds grace and form to the dancers. Take a look at the following photos of the dancers performing a Side-to-Side Balance applying body sway and see what I mean.

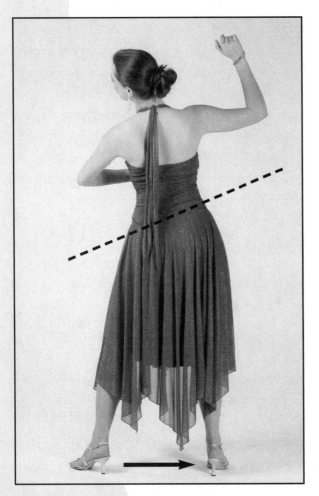

A left body sway during a side step to the right.

Incorrect body sway.

Correct body sway.

Contra Body Motion (CBM)

Although this fundamental dance technique is not exclusive of the waltz, it is an integral part of it. As I mentioned earlier, the waltz is a dance of balance and of boxed movements which can be performed by moving on a straight line forward and back, or by making a turn to the left or to the right on count 1 of a forward or backward step.

In smooth dances, turns danced in closed position are predominant. The tightest turn is a 1/4 turn. It is also the easiest to lead and to follow. The widest turn is a half turn as in the Viennese Waltz turns. It is the most advanced of waltz turns. When first learning turning moves, male dance students tend to initiate a turn by (first) turning their traveling foot in the direction of the turn they're aiming to make. Then, instead of leading the turn with their body, they tend to use their arms to move their partners in the direction toward which they are turning. This is not only incorrect, but it also results in the type of lead that very few women can follow.

You might recall a previous statement I've made: "The body always moves first!"

While adhering to this rule is a man's key to a good leading technique, its application is of the utmost importance during the initiation of almost all turning moves, especially of box turning moves. This technique is referred to as Contra Body Motion (CBM).

Chances are that you've never heard of Contra Body Motion before, although it's been a part of the way you've been moving ever since you took your first walking step. During our normal way of walking or running, we swing our arms and shoulders in opposition to the foot we're moving. When you step forward with your left, it is your right arm that swings freely forward. Actually, it is not just your right arm that swings forward, but the right half of your entire upper body. Your body naturally moves this way. If you don't think so, try walking same-leg same-arm. So men, when you lead, you'll want to use this same motion and lead with your whole body.

Contra Body Motion is so important a leading/following technique that I've devoted some time to it during the opening segments of your DVD waltz chapter. Learning to apply Contra Body Motion is important for both partners, but more so for the man than for the woman. Correct application of Contra Body Motion, especially in any of the smooth dances, is what will make any man the type of dancer every woman can follow with ease.

To my students, I define Contra Body Motion as a gradual twisting of the upper torso in the direction you plan to lead a Closed Dance Position turn. As an example, think of how you direct the steering wheel of a car as you're about to turn a corner: You reposition your hand placing it higher up on your steering wheel and start turning it to the left. But if you think of it, you're also guiding your left hand with not only your right shoulder, but also with the entire upper right side of your body as you're making the turn. Once the turn is completed, you are back seating upright and your right hand automatically goes lower on your steering wheel.

Take a look at this bird's eye illustration showing the upper body as a shoulder-to-shoulder horizontal line placed behind two footprints.

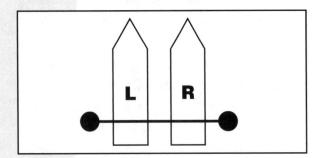

Then, look at the second illustration and see how the line has changed as the left foot commences to make a left turning forward curve.

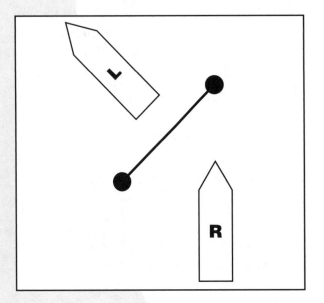

And, last, how the horizontal line is back to its original relation to the feet once the pattern has been completed.

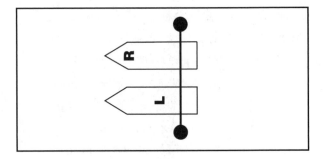

The exact same process, but in reverse, takes place during the back turning portion of the dance pattern which is the woman's mirror opposite of the first three steps of the dance pattern.

Waltz Dance Pattern No. 1

Basic Balance A (Forward and Back)

TIMING: 3/4

RHYTHM: Accented "1" count.

NUMBER OF COUNTS: 6

NUMBER OF ACTUAL STEPS: 2

NUMBER OF ACTUAL FOOT MOVEMENTS: 4

CHARACTERISTICS: On count 2, the moving foot closes next to the supporting foot and taps. There's no weight change in a tap step.

DANCE TIP:

Men, unless your partner is looking down at your feet as you start to dance—instead of looking at your admiring eyes—she won't have a clue of what you're about to do or what direction you're about to move in. Partner dancing is all about communicating through the body —not just the hands.

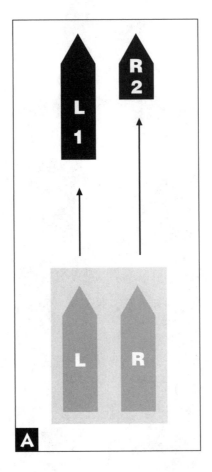

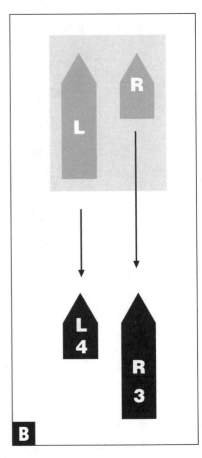

Box	Step	Count	M—Foot Placement	DP
A	1	1	Fwd with LF	CL
	2	2	Tap RF next to LF (NWC)	
	Hold	3	No foot movement	
B	3	4	Bk with RF	
	4	5	Tap LF next to RF (NWC)	
	Hold	6	No foot movement	

Waltz Dance Pattern No. 1

W

Basic Balance A (Forward and Back)

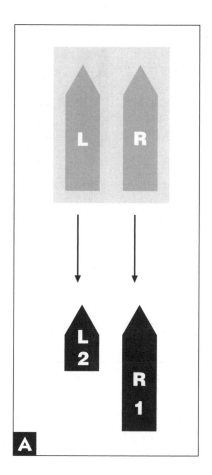

A

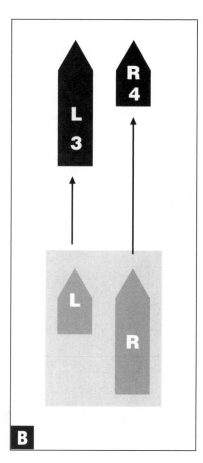

B

TIMING: 3/4
RHYTHM: Accented "1" count.
NUMBER OF COUNTS: 6
NUMBER OF ACTUAL STEPS: 2
NUMBER OF ACTUAL FOOT MOVEMENTS: 4
CHARACTERISTICS: On count 2, the moving foot closes next to the supporting foot and taps. There's no weight change in a tap step.

Box	Step	Count	W—Foot Placement	DP
A	1	1	Bk with RF	CL
	2	2	Tap LF next to RF (NWC)	
	Hold	3	No foot movement	
B	3	4	Fwd with LF	
	4	5	Tap RF next to LF (NWC)	
	Hold	6	No foot movement	

M

Waltz Dance Pattern No. 2

Basic Balance B (Turning Left)

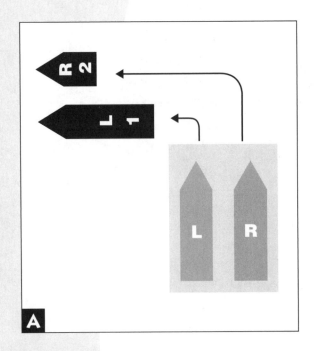

A

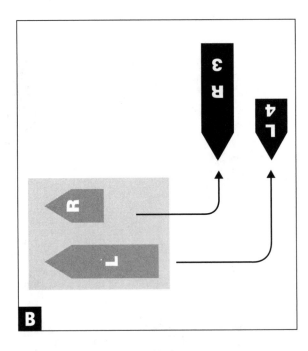

B

DANCE TIP:

In the Balance B, the man turns 1/4 to the left (a toe-out foot movement) on every forward step.

TIMING: 3/4
RHYTHM: Accented "1" count.
NUMBER OF COUNTS: 6
NUMBER OF ACTUAL STEPS: 2
NUMBER OF ACTUAL FOOT MOVEMENTS: 4
CHARACTERISTICS: Contra Body Motion (CBM) is applied to initiate every turning foot placement.

Box	Step	Count	M—Foot Placement	DP
A	1	1	Fwd with LF (toe-out 1/4 Trn L) CBM	CL
	2	2	Tap RF next to LF	
	Hold	3	No movement	
B	3	4	Bk with RF (toe-in 1/4 Trn L) CMB	
	4	5	Tap LF next to RF	
	Hold	6	No movement	

Waltz Dance Pattern No. 2

Basic Balance B (Turning Left)

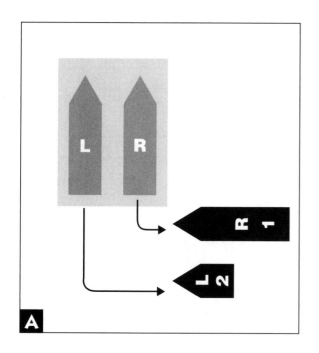

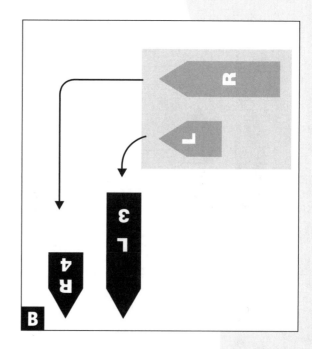

DANCE TIP:

In the Balance B, the woman turns 1/4 to the left (a toe-in foot movement) on every back step.

Box	Step	Count	W—Foot Placement	DP
A	1	1	Bk with RF	CL
			(toe-in 1/4 Trn L) CBM	
	2	2	Tap LF next to RF	
	Hold	3	No movement	
B	3	4	Fwd with LF	
			(toe-out 1/4 Trn L) CBM	
	4	5	Tap RF next to LF	
	Hold	6	No movement	

TIMING: 3/4

RHYTHM: Accented "1" count.

NUMBER OF COUNTS: 6

NUMBER OF ACTUAL STEPS: 2

NUMBER OF ACTUAL FOOT MOVEMENTS: 4

CHARACTERISTICS: On count 2, the moving foot closes next to the supporting foot and taps. There's no weight change in a tap step.

Waltz Dance Pattern No. 3

The Side-to-Side Balance

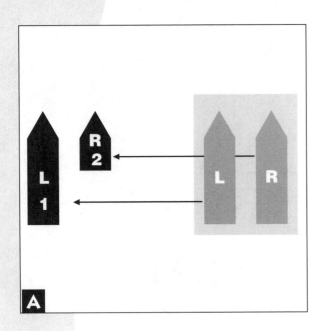

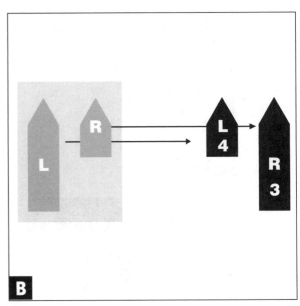

TIMING: 3/4
RHYTHM: Accented "1" count.
NUMBER OF COUNTS: 6
NUMBER OF ACTUAL STEPS: 2
NUMBER OF ACTUAL FOOT MOVEMENTS: 4
CHARACTERISTICS: Body sway is the characteristic styling move of the side-to-side balance. However, it can be done without any sway at all.

Box	Step	Count	M—Foot Placement	DP
A	1	1	Sd with LF	CL
	2	2	Tap RF next to LF (NWC)	
	Hold	3	No foot movement	
B	3	4	Sd with RF	
	4	5	Tap LF next to RF (NWC)	
	Hold	6	No foot movement	

Waltz Dance Pattern No. 3

The Side-to-Side Balance

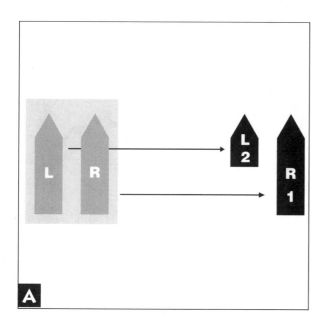

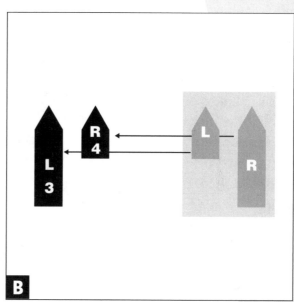

Box	Step	Count	W—Foot Placement	DP
A	1	1	Sd with RF	CL
	2	2	Tap LF next to RF (NWC)	
	Hold	3	No foot movement	
B	3	4	Sd with LF	
	4	5	Tap RF next to LF (NWC)	
	Hold	6	No foot movement	

Timing: 3/4

Rhythm: Accented "1" count.

Number of Counts: 6

Number of Actual Steps: 2

Number of Actual Foot Movements: 4

Characteristics: Body sway is the characteristic styling move of the side-to-side balance. However, it can be done without any sway at all.

Waltz Dance Pattern No. 4

The Fifth Position Rock/Breaks

TIMING: 3/4

RHYTHM: Accented "1" count.

NUMBER OF COUNTS: 6

NUMBER OF ACTUAL STEPS: 6

CHARACTERISTICS: A Fifth Position Break is one during which partners dance a rocking step on counts 2 and 3, placing one foot behind the other, forming the shape of an "L" with their feet. The term Fifth Position comes from one of the classic ballet's five positions of the feet.

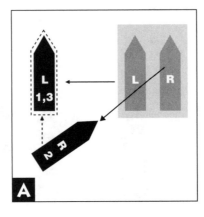

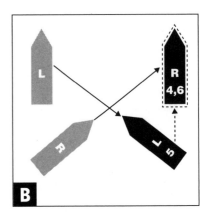

Box	Step	Count	M—Foot Placement	DP
A	1	1	Sd with LF	CL
	2	2	X RF behind LF (toe-out 1/8 Trn R)	RO
	3	3	Fwd In-Pl with LF*	CL
B	4	4	Sd with RF	
	5	5	X LF behind RF (toe-out 1/8 Trn L)	LO
	6	6	Fwd In-Pl with RF	CL

*In-Pl steps denoted by dotted lines.

DANCE TIP:

As the feet cross in the Fifth Position break, let the head turn over the shoulder corresponding to the foot that's being crossed—head turns left as the left foot crosses behind the right foot.

DANCE TIP:

The alternating changes in dance positions make this simple dance pattern a little more challenging. The key to leading this pattern, and to its changes in dance positions, is in the hips. As man takes the side step, he must bring his left hip forward toward his partner's right hip at the same time that he loosens his right hand hold. This allows both partners to open up their right (for man) and left (for woman) sides away from each other thus making it easier for both to cross one foot behind the other as in Step 3. For step 5, reverse the process by leading with the right hip.

Waltz Dance Pattern No. 4

W

The Fifth Position Rock/Breaks

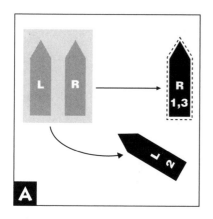

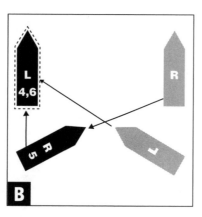

TIMING: 3/4
RHYTHM: Accented "1" count.
NUMBER OF COUNTS: 6
NUMBER OF ACTUAL STEPS: 6
CHARACTERISTICS: A Fifth Position Balance is one during which partners dance a rocking step on counts 2 and 3, placing one foot behind the other, forming the shape of an "L" with their feet. The term Fifth Position comes from one of the classic ballet's five positions of the feet.

Box	Step	Count	W—Foot Placement	DP
A	1	1	Sd with RF	CL
	2	2	X LF behind RF (toe-out 1/8 Trn L)	RO
	3	3	Fwd In-Pl with RF	CL
B	4	4	Sd with LF	
	5	5	X RF behind LF (toe-out 1/8 Trn R)	LO
	6	6	Fwd In-Pl with LF	CL

DANCE TIP:

As the feet cross in the Fifth Position break, let the head turn over the shoulder corresponding to the foot that's being crossed—head turns left as the left foot crosses behind the right foot.

Waltz Dance Pattern No. 5

The Waltz Box Step

TIMING: 3/4

RHYTHM: Accented "1" count.

NUMBER OF COUNTS: 6

NUMBER OF ACTUAL STEPS: 6

CHARACTERISTICS: In all box-like patterns during which a moving foot (the traveling foot) closes right next to the weight-bearing foot (the supporting foot), an immediate shift of the body's weight (WC) takes place from the supporting foot to the just closing foot, freeing the now-free foot to move onto the next step that follows.

DANCE TIP:

There's no way to avoid it. Without learning to dance a good waltz step, any waltz will end up looking much like a foxtrot.

The good old Box Step is the magical step. Within its simple geometric configuration you can learn so much about social dancing, both in the smooth and rhythm categories. I often tell students, *Master a Box Step and you'll not only learn to do just about anything you'll ever need to do to shine on a dance floor, but you will have learned all the important techniques and rules of social dancing.*

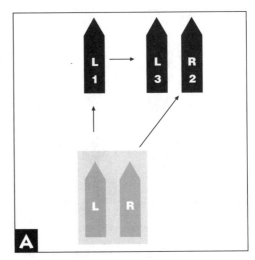

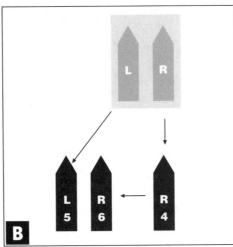

Box	Step	Count	M—Foot Placement	DP
A	1	1	Fwd with LF	CL
	2	2	Sd with RF	
	3	3	Close LF to RF (WC)	
B	4	4	Bk with RF	
	5	5	Sd with LF	
	6	6	Close RF to LF (WC)	

Waltz Dance Pattern No. 5

W

The Waltz Box Step

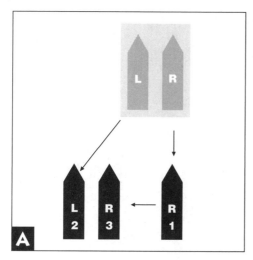

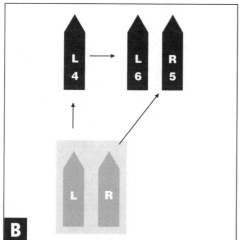

TIMING: 3/4
RHYTHM: Accented "1" count.
NUMBER OF COUNTS: 6
NUMBER OF ACTUAL STEPS: 6
CHARACTERISTICS: In all box-like patterns during which a moving foot (the traveling foot) closes right next to the weight-bearing foot (the supporting foot), an immediate shift of the body's weight (WC) takes place from the supporting foot to the just closing foot, freeing the now-free foot to move onto the next step that follows.

DANCE TIP:

Please remember that, especially in smooth dances, we neither use our arms to push a partner into moving nor use them to pull them into a pattern. The body initiates all movements. It is the center of communication between dance partners. It is what makes two people dance as one. Our feet are the vehicle through which we move from one step to the other, but it is the body that moves us.

Don't let your feet get ahead of your body. When that happens you're looking for trouble by stepping or being stepped on by your partner's feet.

Box	Step	Count	W—Foot Placement	DP
A	1	1	Bk with RF	CL
	2	2	Sd with LF	
	3	3	Close RF to LF (WC)	
B	4	4	Fwd with LF	
	5	5	Sd with RF	
	6	6	Close LF to RF (WC)	

M Waltz Dance Pattern No. 6

The Left Turning Box Step

TIMING: 3/4

RHYTHM: Accented "1" count.

NUMBER OF COUNTS: 12

NUMBER OF ACTUAL STEPS: 12

CHARACTERISTICS: Ideally, you want to dance two full turning box steps, turning 1/4 to the left on each half box in order to end up on the same spot where you started.

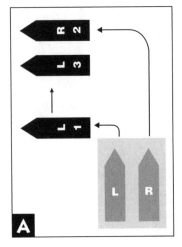

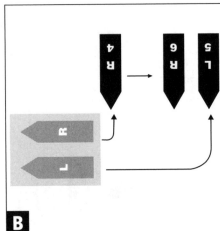

DANCE TIP:

During closed Box turns like this one, it is quite common for beginner dancers to find themselves taking too large of a side step. Keep them short, especially as you start practicing this move. Even during turning moves, the feet should be kept under the frame of the dancers' bodies. This is especially important during the back half of a turning box when the feet are toeing in to make the turn.

Box	Step	Count	M—Foot Placement	DP
A	1	1	Fwd with LF	CL
			(toe-out 1/4 Trn L) CBM	
	2	2	Sd with RF	
	3	3	Close LF to RF (WC)	
B	4	4	Bk with RF	
			(toe-in 1/4 Trn L) CBM	
	5	5	Sd with LF	
	6	6	Close RF to LF (WC)	
	7-12	7-12	Repeat steps 1-6	

DVD LESSON:

Your DVD waltz chapter features a one-on-one segment that links the Balance steps and the Box turns.

Waltz Dance Pattern No. 6

W

The Left Turning Box Step

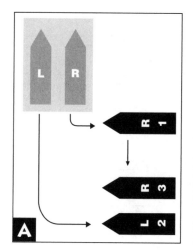

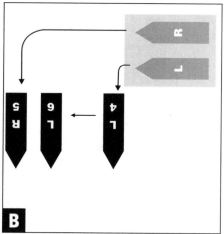

TIMING: 3/4

RHYTHM: Accented "1" count.

NUMBER OF COUNTS: 12

NUMBER OF ACTUAL STEPS: 12

CHARACTERISTICS: Ideally, you want to dance two full turning box steps, turning 1/4 to the left on each half box in order to end up on the same spot where you started.

Box	Step	Count	W—Foot Placement	DP
A	1	1	Bk with RF (toe–in 1/4 Trn L) CBM	CL
	2	2	Sd with LF	
	3	3	Close RF to LF (WC)	
B	4	4	Fwd with LF (toe-out 1/4 Trn L) CBM	
	5	5	Sd with RF	
	6	6	Close LF to RF (WC)	
	7–12	7–12	Repeat steps 1-6	

DANCE TIP:

You've already learned the two principal components of the Turning Box: the Forward and Back Turning Balances and the Square Box. In the Balances, you learned about the use of Contra Body Movement as the body movement that initiates all close dance position turns. In the Box Step, you learned the number one rule of social dancing foot placements: *Unless otherwise indicated, whenever a traveling foot closes next to a supporting foot there is an immediate change of weight that takes place from the supporting foot to the traveling foot.*

Now, let's go for it.

Showy Dance Moves for the Bride and Groom

The Oversway

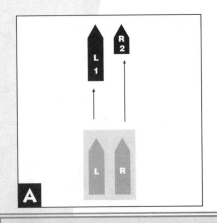

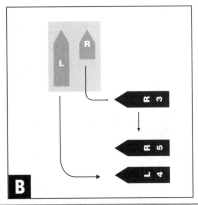

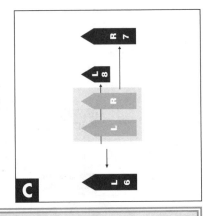

DANCE TIP:

The man leads the Oversway by turning his right hip and shoulder toward his partner, forming a picture with both of their upper bodies. To make this movement even more stylized, partners can look over their shoulder away from each other for a couple of counts then back toward each other before coming out of the movement with a side–hesitation balance. Believe me, you'll hear the applause and the click of cameras. Men, on Step 6, as the weight shifts onto the right foot, let the right knee bend a little more. Doing this will let your partner feel a more accented shift of weight. It will also allow you to take a longer and smoother side step (a left foot lunge) into the actual oversway on Step 7.

TIMING: 3/4

NUMBER OF COUNTS: 12

NUMBER OF ACTUAL STEPS: 8

CHARACTERISTICS: An Oversway is a "picture" movement that's danced with the upper body following a large side step, called a "Lunge," on which the body of both partners stands on a bent knee. The free leg is extended out to the side with their feet pointed. This dance pattern combines a portion of the Forward Balance with the back half of a Turning Box and ends with a side-hesitation balance.

Box	Step	Count	M—Foot Placement	DP
A	1	1	Fwd with LF	CL
	2	2	Tap RF to LF (NWC)	
	Hold	3	No movement	
B	3	4	Bk with RF	
			(toe-in 1/4 Trn L)	
	4	5	Sd with LF	
C	5	6	Close RF to LF (WC)	
	6	1	Sd with LF (Lunge)	
	Hold	2	Oversway. Hold position	
	Hold	3	Oversway. Hold position	
	7	4	Sd with RF	
	8	5	Tap LF to RF (NWC)	
	Hold	6	Hold position	

Showy Dance Moves for the Bride and Groom W

The Oversway

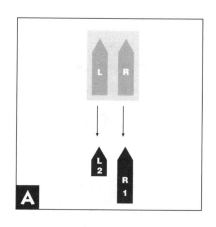

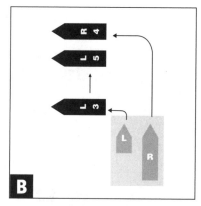

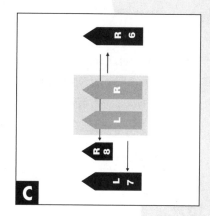

Box	Step	Count	W—Foot Placement	DP
A	1	1	Bk with RF	CL
	2	2	Tap LF to RF (NWC)	
B	Hold	3	No movement	
	3	4	Fwd with LF (toe-out 1/4 Trn L)	
	4	5	Sd with RF	
	5	6	Close LF to RF (WC)	
C	6	1	Side with RF (Lunge)	
	Hold	2	Oversway Hold position	
	Hold	3	Oversway. Hold position	
	7	4	Sd with LF	
	8	5	Tap RF to LF (NWC)	
	Hold	6	Hold position	

DANCE TIP:

Women, on Step 6, as you feel your partner's weight shift, let your right leg take a longer side step. Then, as your partner guides you to shift your weight onto your right leg (on Step 7), settle your weight and balance well over it before turning your left shoulder and facing away from your partner.

Showy Dance Moves for the Bride and Groom

The Underarm Turn

For the man, this is a very easy pattern to dance. All he does is dance four measures of a Box Step (12 counts) while leading his partner to turn under his left hand on the back half of his first Box Step. Then, on the back half of his second Box Step he brings his partner back into CL Dance Position.

DANCE TIP:

To lead the UA Turn the man has to release his right hand hold on Step 4. Then, on Step 5 he raises his left hand indicating to his partner that he wishes for her to dance an underarm turn. While his partner continues dancing a wide open, full circle, to the right, the man continues dancing a Box Step. On Step 11, he takes his partner back into CL Dance Position to complete his last half of a Box Step.

DVD LESSON:

Your DVD waltz chapter features a one-on-one segment that links these last two dance patterns.

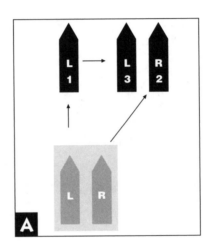

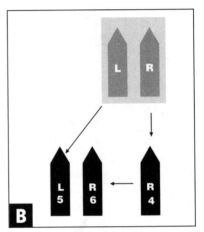

Box	Step	Count	M—Foot Placement	DP
A	1	1	Fwd with LF	CL
	2	2	Sd with RF	
	3	3	Close LF to RF (WC)	
B	4	4	Bk with RF	1HH
	5	5	Sd with LF	
	6	6	Close RF to LF (WC)	
	7–12	Repeat Steps 1–6		

Showy Dance Moves for the Bride and Groom **W**

The Underarm Turn

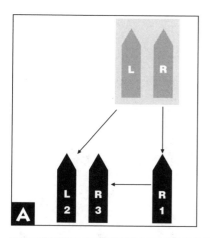

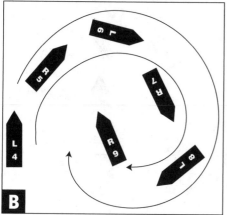

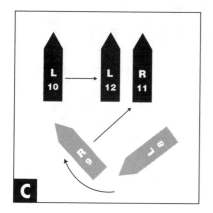

Box	Step	Count	W—Foot Placement	DP
A	1	1	Bk with RF	CL
	2	2	Sd with LF	
	3	3	Close RF to LF (WC)	
B	4	4	Fwd with LF	1HH
	5	5	Fwd with RF (toe-out 1/4 Trn to R)	
	6	6	Fwd with LF (continue R circle)	
	7	1	Fwd with RF (continue R circle)	
	8	2	Fwd with LF (continue R circle)	
	9	3	Fwd with RF (continue R circle)	
	10	4	Fwd with LF (completes R circle)	
C	11	5	Sd with RF	CL
	12	6	Close LF to RF (WC)	

DANCE TIP:

For the woman, this pattern requires that she continue dancing a series of seven continuous forward steps, forming a circle. She returns to her partner on the seventh forward walking step (Step 10), catching up with her partner to complete the last two steps of a Box Step.

Showy Dance Moves for the Bride and Groom

The Underarm Turn

The man raises his left arm on Step 4 to lead his partner into the underarm turn.

On Step 5, the woman starts dancing a tight, 6-step circle to the right under her partner's left hand.

Showy Dance Moves for the Bride and Groom

The Underarm Turn

On Step 7, the woman continues her turn. This dance pattern makes for a great photo op.

Chapter 7

The Foxtrot

Various dance articles and publications credit the "fox trot" to an American vaudevillian, Harry Fox, who "trotted" to ragtime music on a New York theater stage in the early 1900s. But the foxtrot we know today is a far cry from anything Mr. Fox might have danced.

Historically, all social dances have evolved from a combination of original works in music and choreography by artists of the music and dance world, respectively. Few dances have evolved into their present format in short years. It is therefore quite possible that today's foxtrot is as much a part of the work of popular exhibition dancers of the early nineties (such as Vernon and Irene Castle), as it is of countless ballroom dance teams and master teachers who came into the dance scene much later.

Regardless, the foxtrot is as American as apple pie. It is the signature dance of ceremonial events—inauguration balls, award ceremonies, etc. It is also a dance that has split into various dance styles and tempos. Its most elemental dance pattern, the side-to-side rocking step, can be easily danced to a variety of tunes and tempos that include ballads, blues, rock 'n' roll, pop and even slow tempo swing.

Among the many names by which this two-step, side-to-side, basic foxtrot move is known, the one I get the biggest kick out of is "the businessman's

bounce." Also called the "two-step," it consists of one side step (to the left for the man and to the right for the woman), danced to two beats of music (a Slow count), and followed by a second side step (to the right for the man and to the left for the woman), also danced to two beats of music. Recognize it? Most likely, you do. And because just about every foxtrot, ballad, slow swing, rock or pop tune is written in 4/4 timing (four beats to every musical measure), staying on the beat while only "bobbing" from one side to the next is so very easy to do, especially if you are wearing new shoes, or trying out a formal tuxedo suit or a floor-length wedding gown, or if you didn't spend enough time practicing the foxtrot steps featured in this chapter.

Whether you "businessman bounce," "two-step," or learn the correct way to dance some very simple standard foxtrot patterns, foxtrot-danceable melodies abound. At weddings here are some of the ones most often used for the "first dance" or the "father-daughter dance": "Nothing Compares to You," by Sinead O'Connor, "Unforgettable" by Natalie Cole, "Circle of Life" by Elton John, "Just in Time" by Tony Bennet and "From This Moment" by Shania Twain. All have a slow tempo and very meaningful lyrics. But, old-fashioned as I may sound, there's nothing that compares to the feeling one gets when dancing a foxtrot to Frank Sinatra's rendition of "New York, New York," second only to Liza Minnelli's own rendition.

Today, most ballroom dance studios teach two styles of foxtrot, the American and the International. In the American style, social-level dance patterns consist mostly of combinations of forward, back, and side steps during which the feet come together shifting weight from a supporting foot to a traveling foot, forming box-like figures that do not travel a lot and that can be performed in gradual turns, ranging from 1/8 to 1/2 turns to the left or to the right. Within the social level, dance patterns are often grouped into beginner, intermediate, and advanced levels. The beginner, or partnering, level consists of the basic, or signature, dance patterns of a dance. The intermediate and advanced levels generally consist of variations of the signature patterns during which students learn additional dance positions and longer dance patterns.

Beyond the social level, foxtrot dance patterns can move along the line of dance as well as into and out of the center of the dance floor. Turning moves are danced without the feet coming together and shifting weight which allows dancers to connect different dance patterns into long sequences. This level is often referred to as "continuity style foxtrot."

In the International style, many foxtrot dance patterns, including those in a beginner's level, resemble many of the American continuity style dance patterns, crisscrossing the dance floor in a variety of smooth, gliding, turns that often lead dancers into "picture poses."

Although all dance styles and their respective dances have their own "social level," it is the American social level that's not only the easiest to learn, to lead, and to follow, but also the most fun to do at parties and on crowded dance floors.

Fundamental Elements of the Foxtrot

FOOTWORK

The dance patterns of the foxtrot generally consist of long forward and backward strides and short side steps. With less than a handful of exceptions, forward-moving steps are always taken with a heel lead just like during a regular walking step. Backward-moving steps are always taken with a toe/ball lead.

It is both the strength and the flexibility of our own ankles and feet that allow us to gradually "roll" the body's weight, starting from the heel of the moving foot to the center of the foot and then onto the ball and toes.

Conversely, it is from the inside edge of the supporting foot that a push-off action takes place prior to the taking of a side step. However, a sideward push-off action is never as strong because the distance between side steps is that much shorter than the distance between forward and backward moving steps.

There is also another reason for the foxtrot's characteristic heel/toe lead. That reason is the dance's own musical beat or count structure, its timing, and how it applies to the individual placement of the feet within a dance pattern.

TIMING AND RHYTHM

Foxtrot dance music follows a 4/4 format: four counts to a measure of music. In each measure of music there are two accented beats: the first and third beats. The first beat, the "one" beat is the most accented of the four. Both the first and the third beat are each called "down beats." The second and fourth beat are each called "up beats." Dance patterns are choreographed to fit an even distribution of musical beats and measures. Generally, there are two to four measures per dance pattern. The American foxtrot is danced at a tempo of 30 to 32 measures-per-minute (MPM). The foxtrot can also be danced to many swing and pop tunes with faster tempos that range between 32 and 38 MPM.

Rhythm refers to the manner in which musical counts are distributed per every foot placement or individual step. Rhythm is as much a part of the individual placement of the feet as it is of the movement of the entire body while it moves from one foot placement to the next. One beat per step makes that step a quick step (Q). Two beats per step makes that step a slow step (S).

Foxtrot dance patterns are choreographed according to two main rhythmic structures: SQQ (four beats total), SSQQ (six beats total), or a combination of SQQ and SSQQ rhythms.

DANCE STANCE, FRAME, POSITIONS, AND HOLDS

All foxtrot dance patterns start with the feet placed slightly apart. The man's weight is on the right foot. The woman's weight is on the left foot. Dancers stand tall, keeping their knees slightly bent and with their body's weight toward the front half of their feet. As it applies to all smooth dances, partners maintain an upright body position with their bodies in contact and with their arms forming a triangular figure: the dance frame. The woman's upper torso arches slightly to her left, allowing her partner to have a clear view over her right shoulder.

Partners dancing a foxtrot.

BASIC RHYTHMS OF DANCE PATTERNS

Beats/Counts in Rhythmic Groups
Slow Quick Quick (SQQ):

1 2 3 4 5 6 7 8   1 2 3 4 5 6 7 8
S   Q Q S   Q Q   S   Q Q S   Q Q

Slow Slow Quick Quick (SSQQ):

1 2 3 4 5 6   7 8 1 2 3 4   5 6 7 8 1 2   3 4 5 6 7 8
S S Q Q   S S Q Q   S S Q Q   S S Q Q

DANCE POSITIONS

Closed Dance Position (CL)

In a Closed Dance Position (CL), the man places his partner off to his right. The right side of the woman's body is placed off to the right of an imaginary vertical line that runs down the center of his body. Her upper body maintains a left-leaning curve that starts at her lower spine and ends at the crown of the head. Her neck must show an elongated, graceful line, and her head will have a slight tilt to the left. Her correct dance stance will allow her partner to have a clear frontal view of other couples on the dance floor.

Another important element while in a Closed Dance Position is the actual position of the partners' feet in relation to each other. Remember that the woman should stand off to the right of her partner, rather than facing him squarely, so that her feet are located in parallel lanes with his feet. Maintaining this parallel foot placement is what will keep partners from stepping on each other's toes while dancing in closed dance position.

The position of dance partner's arms is referred to as the "dance frame." The elbows are held out and to the sides of the body, as if resting on an imaginary horizontal line that runs across the middle of a dancer's shoulder blades, connecting the elbows. Keeping the arms in the correct framed position does take time and practice.

The perfect Closed Dance Position dance frame.

A sloppy-looking dance frame.

A graceful-looking dance frame.

The man's left forearm is held up from its elbow at a 90-degree angle.

The left hand and wrist are held firmly and in direct line with the forearm.

The heel of the man's right hand is placed on the woman's back, just under her left shoulder blade, and with fingers closed and stacked on top of each other. Men do not lead with the fingers of the right hand. They lead with the entire hand, moving it slightly from its wrist as if it were a hinge.

While the man's arms are placed under the woman's arms, the woman is never to think of them as a place of rest. She must hold her own. The role of the man's dance frame is to guide his partner on the dance floor but not to carry his partner on it.

Her left forearm is placed over the man's right upper arm. Her left wrist is generally placed just under the seam of the man's right jacket sleeve, and her fingers should be kept close together and cupping the man's right shoulder.

The palm of her right hand is placed against the palm of her partner's left hand with fingers draping over the outer edge of his index finger in a soft clasp.

The man's dance frame.

The woman's dance frame.

Left Open Dance Position (LO)

The Left Open Dance Position (LO) is also referred to as a Promenade Position because both partners move in the same direction: The man is moving or walking forward to his left. The woman is following along moving or walking forward to her right. During Left Open Dance Position, partners maintain a parallel dance frame.

Partners dancing in Left Open (Promenade) Dance Position.

DANCE PATTERN BUILDING BLOCKS

The pattern building blocks of the foxtrot are the Forward, Back and Side Balance/Rocking Steps and the Box Step. A Balance step consists of just one step taken forward, back or side on count 1 followed by a tap step on count 2. The rhythm of one balance step is Slow (S). Tap steps are followed by another step using the same foot as the tapping foot. Most Balance steps are followed by either the forward or the back half of a Box Step.

Box Step:

Step	M & W—Foot Placement	DP
1	Fwd with LF	CL
2	Sd with RF	
3	Close LF to RF (WC)	
4	Bk with RF	
5	Sd with LF	
6	Close RF to LF (WC)	

CHARACTERISTIC STYLE OF THE FOXTROT

The foxtrot is characterized by a gentle, almost cushion-like bounce, which results from the constant, alternating, flexing, and straightening (but not locking) of the knees that take place on every step.

Forward and back traveling steps are longer than side steps. When the moving foot must travel directly to the side from a forward or back direction, it should brush past the supporting foot. This characteristic is referred to as "follow through." It is an important dance element to know and practice, especially for beginner students, because it forces the moving foot to stay under the body's frame at all times rather than moving ahead of the body.

M Foxtrot Dance Pattern No. 1

The Two-Step Basic A (Side-to-Side)

TIMING: 4/4
RHYTHM: SSQQ
NUMBER OF COUNTS: 12
NUMBER OF STEPS: 6
CHARACTERISTICS: Short side steps keeping knees flexible throughout.

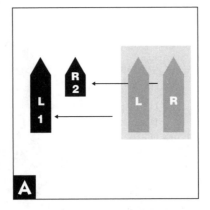

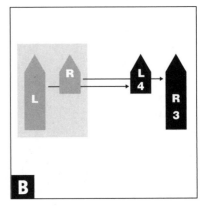

This is the simplest of all foxtrot patterns and one that's been known by several names including "the two-step" and "the businessman's bounce" because it not only consists of just a two-step sequence but it is also one which the most two-left-feet business men can easily get away with at corporate parties.

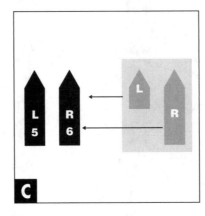

Box	Step	Count	Rhythm	M—Foot Placement	DP
A	1	1	S	Sd with LF	CL
	2	2		Tap RF to LF (NWC)	
B	3	3	S	Sd with RF	
	4	4		Tap LF to RF (NWC)	
C	5	5	Q	Sd with LF	
	6	6	Q	Close RF to LF (WC)	
	Repeat steps 1–6				

Foxtrot Dance Pattern No. 1

W

The Two-Step Basic A (Side-to-Side)

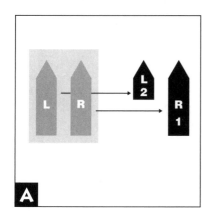

A

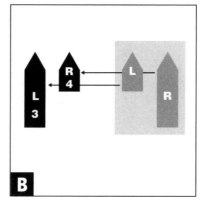

B

TIMING: 4/4
RHYTHM: SSQQ
NUMBER OF COUNTS: 12
NUMBER OF STEPS: 6
CHARACTERISTICS: Short side steps keeping knees flexible throughout.

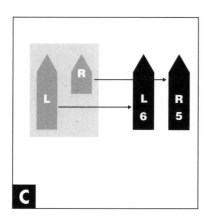

C

BOX	STEP	COUNT	RHYTHM	W—FOOT PLACEMENT	DP
A	1	1	S	Sd with RF	CL
	2	2		Tap LF to RF (NWC)	
B	3	3	S	Sd with LF	
	4	4		Tap RF to LF (NWC)	
C	5	5	Q	Sd with RF	
	6	6	Q	Close LF to RF (WC)	
	Repeat steps 1–6				

Foxtrot Dance Pattern No. 2

The Two-Step Basic B (Forward and Back)

TIMING: 4/4
RHYTHM: SSQQ
NUMBER OF COUNTS: 6
NUMBER OF STEPS: 6
CHARACTERISTICS: Longer forward and back strides but shorter side strides. This pattern combines a forward/back balance component with the second half of a Box Step.

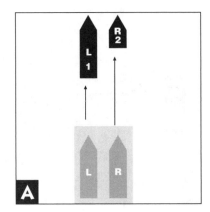

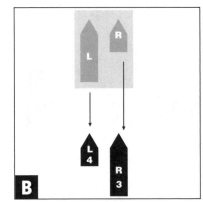

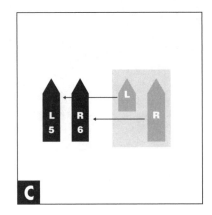

Box	Step	Count	Rhythm	M—Foot Placement	DP
A	1	1	S	Fwd with LF	CL
	2	2		Tap RF to LF (NWC)	
B	3	3	S	Bk with RF	
	4	4		Tap LF to RF (NWC)	
C	5	5	Q	Sd with LF	
	6	6	Q	Close RF to LF (WC)	

Foxtrot Dance Pattern No. 2

W

The Two-Step Basic B (Forward and Back)

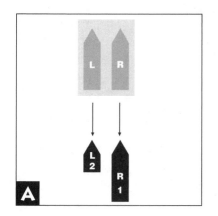

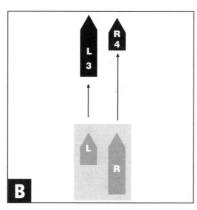

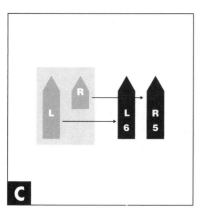

TIMING: 4/4
RHYTHM: SSQQ
NUMBER OF COUNTS: 6
NUMBER OF STEPS: 6
CHARACTERISTICS: Longer forward and back strides but shorter side strides. This pattern combines a forward/back balance component with the second half of a Box Step.

Box	Step	Count	Rhythm	W—Foot Placement	DP
A	1	1	S	Bk with RF	CL
	2	2		Tap LF to RF (NWC)	
B	3	3	S	Fwd with LF	
	4	4		Tap RF to LF (NWC)	
C	5	5	Q	Sd with RF	
	6	6	Q	Close LF to RF (WC)	

Foxtrot Dance Pattern No. 3

The Two-Step Basic C (Left Turning)

TIMING: 4/4
RHYTHM: SSQQ
NUMBER OF COUNTS: 6
NUMBER OF STEPS: 6
CHARACTERISTICS: This variation calls for a 1/4 turn to the left to be danced on Step 1. For a smooth performance of any type of turn in CL dance position, CBM should be simultaneously applied to the foot on which the turn is being made.

DVD LESSON:

Your DVD foxtrot chapter contains a one-on-one segment featuring the above patterns.

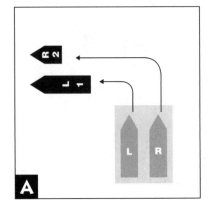
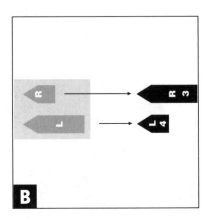
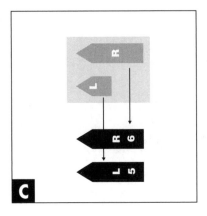

Box	Step	Count	Rhythm	M—Foot Placement	DP
A	1	1	S	Fwd with LF (toe-in 1/4 Trn L) CBM	CL
	2	2		Tap RF to LF (NWC)	
B	3	3	S	Bk with RF	
	4	4		Tap LF to RF (NWC)	
C	5	5	Q	Sd with LF	
	6	6	Q	Close RF to LF (WC)	

Foxtrot Dance Pattern No. 3

W

The Two-Step Basic C (Left Turning)

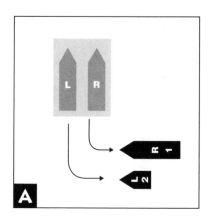

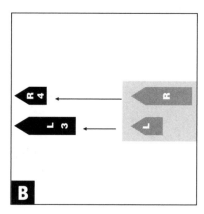

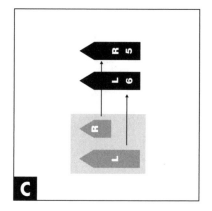

TIMING: 4/4
RHYTHM: SSQQ
NUMBER OF COUNTS: 6
NUMBER OF STEPS: 6
CHARACTERISTICS: This variation calls for a 1/4 turn to the right (opposite of the man's) to be danced on Step 1. For a smooth performance of any type of turn in CL dance position, CBM should be simultaneously applied to the foot on which the turn is being made.

DVD LESSON:

Your DVD foxtrot chapter contains a one-on-one segment featuring the above patterns.

Box	Step	Count	Rhythm	W—Foot Placement	DP
A	1	1	S	Bk with RF (toe-in 1/4 Trn L) CBM	CL
	2	2		Tap LF to RF (NWC)	
B	3	3	S	Fwd with LF	
	4	4		Tap RF to LF (NWC)	
C	5	5	Q	Sd with RF	
	6	6	Q	Close LF to RF (WC)	

Foxtrot Dance Pattern No. 4

The Foxtrot Box Step A

TIMING: 4/4
RHYTHM: SQQ
NUMBER OF COUNTS: 8
NUMBER OF STEPS: 6
CHARACTERISTICS: Follow through of the moving foot when going from a forward or back movement onto a side movement.

DANCE TIP:

There are two halves to a Box Step: the forward and the back half. Each consists of three steps for the man and the woman, each half being the mirror opposite of the other.

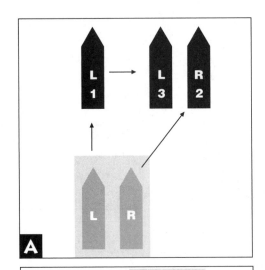

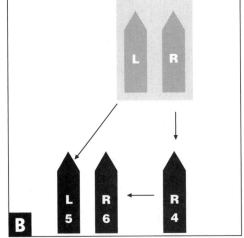

Box	Step	Count	Rhythm	M—Foot Placement	DP
A	1	1 & 2	S	Fwd with LF	CL
	2	3	Q	Sd with RF	
	3	4	Q	Close LF to RF (WC)	
B	4	5 & 6	S	Bk with RF	
	5	7	Q	Sd with LF	
	6	8	Q	Close RF to LF (WC)	

Foxtrot Dance Pattern No. 4

The Foxtrot Box Step A

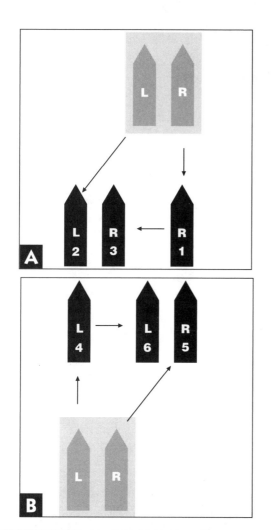

TIMING: 4/4
RHYTHM: SQQ
NUMBER OF COUNTS: 8
NUMBER OF STEPS: 6
CHARACTERISTICS: Follow through of the moving foot when going from a forward or back movement onto a side movement.

DANCE TIP:

Although the count and rhythm is different, the steps for the foxtrot Box Step are the same as for the waltz Box Step.

Box	Step	Count	Rhythm	W—Foot Placement	DP
A	1	1 & 2	S	Bk with RF	CL
	2	3	Q	Sd with LF	
	3	4	Q	Close RF to LF (WC)	
B	4	5 & 6	S	Fwd with LF	
	5	7	Q	Sd with RF	
	6	8	Q	Close LF to RF (WC)	

Foxtrot Dance Pattern No. 5

The Foxtrot Box Step B (Turning)

TIMING: 4/4
RHYTHM: SSQQ
NUMBER OF COUNTS: 12
NUMBER OF STEPS: 12
CHARACTERISTICS: The moving foot follows through when going from a forward or back movement onto a side movement. In a turning Box Step, the first step of the forward half of the Box Step moves forward and outward (toe-out) while the first step of the back half of the Box Step moves back and inward (toe-in). CBM is applied to each turning step. By dancing two full Turning Box Steps, partners will end up back where they started, having completed a full 360-degree turn.

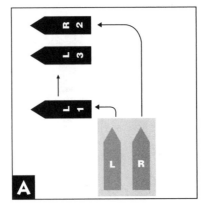

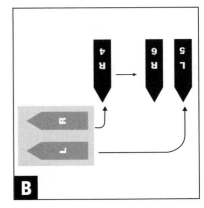

Box	Step	Count	M—Foot Placement	DP
A	1	1	Fwd with LF (toe-out 1/4 Trn L) CBM	CL
	2	2	Sd with RF	
	3	3	Close LF to RF (WC)	
B	4	4	Bk with RF (toe-in 1/4 Trn L) CBM	
	5	5	Sd with LF	
	6	6	Close RF to LF (WC)	
	7–12	7–12	Repeat steps 1–6	

Foxtrot Dance Pattern No. 5

W

The Foxtrot Box Step B (Turning)

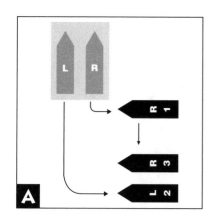

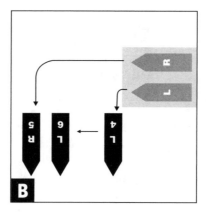

TIMING: 4/4
RHYTHM: SSQQ
NUMBER OF COUNTS: 12
NUMBER OF STEPS: 12
CHARACTERISTICS: The moving foot follows through when going from a forward or back movement onto a side movement. In a turning Box Step, the first step of the forward half of the Box Step moves forward and outward (toe-out) while the first step of the back half of the Box Step moves back and inward (toe-in). CBM is applied to each turning step. By dancing two full Turning Box Steps, partners will end up back where they started, having completed a full 360-degree turn.

Box	Step	Count	W—Foot Placement	DP
A	1	1	Bk with RF	CL
			(toe-in 1/4 Trn L) CBM	
	2	2	Sd with LF	
	3	3	Close RF to LF (WC)	
B	4	4	Fwd with LF	
			(toe-out 1/4 Trn L) CBM	
	5	5	Sd with RF	
	6	6	Close LF to RF (WC)	
	7–12	7–12	Repeat steps 1–6	

Foxtrot Dance Pattern No. 6

The Left Open Basic

TIMING: 4/4

RHYTHM: SSQQ

NUMBER OF COUNTS: 6

NUMBER OF STEPS: 4

CHARACTERISTICS: In this pattern dancers start CL Dance Position but move into LO Dance Position on their first step, pivoting into CL Dance Position on the second step. While the two previous dance patterns, the Two-Step Balances and the Turning Box can be danced anywhere on the dance floor, the Left Open Basic is best danced moving counterclockwise along the LOD.

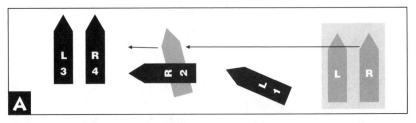

Step	Count	Rhythm	M—Foot Placement	DP
1	1 & 2	S	Fwd with LF (toe-out 1/8 R)	LO
2	3 & 4	S	Fwd with RF (pivot 1/8 R)	LO to CL
3	5	Q	Sd with LF	CL
4	6	Q	RF closes to LF (WC)	

LEADING THE LEFT OPEN BASIC:

Men, getting your partner to change from a closed dance po-sition to a left open dance position and then back to Closed Dance Position takes good leading. But before I give you guys a couple of leading tips, let me remind you of the most important factor in leading any dance pattern, especially when dancing a smooth dance: *Your dance partner is not clairvoyant. It is your mind that first decides what pattern you're going to dance. A fraction of a second later, it is your entire body that must move into action—not your feet, not your left or right hand. Another fraction of a second later, it is your partner that gets the message and follows.*

That being said, here are some leading tips:

1. Just as you are about to move into left open position, use the heel of your right hand to place a little pressure on your partner's back. A little pressure. Don't break her back!

2. At the exact same time, push-off from your supporting foot, opening the left side of your body outward and to the left—the left shoulder leads the movement. That's the point at which your partner will get the message that you've taken her into a different direction. Remember, in smooth dances, women generally move in a direction opposite to their partner's, but seldom in the same direction as their partners.

3. The trickiest movement in this pattern takes place on Step 2 as several things take place during those two counts of music, i.e., crossing the leading foot over the supporting foot, pivoting and regaining close dance position. The dance element that will help both of you achieve all of this without looking like you're both stepping over a pothole is Contra Body Motion. Meaning, as your RF dances past the LF, you should keep the left side of your body as much toward your partner as possible. Doing this will also help you maintain a perfect dance frame and will make it easier for both of you to regain close dance position.

4. Just as you used your hand to apply a little pressure on your partner's back to alert her that you were about to change dance position, you should use the fingers of your right hand to apply a little pressure to let her know you're leading her back into closed dance positit-ion.

Foxtrot Dance Pattern No. 6

The Left Open Basic

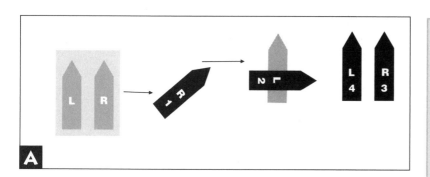

A

TIMING: 4/4
RHYTHM: SSQQ
NUMBER OF COUNTS: 6
NUMBER OF STEPS: 4
CHARACTERISTICS: In this pattern dancers start in CL Dance Position but move into LO Dance Position on their first step, pivoting into CL Dance Position on the second step. While the two previous dance patterns, the Two-Step Balances and the Turning Box can be danced anywhere on the dance floor, the Left Open Basic is best danced moving counterclockwise along the LOD.

STEP	COUNT	RHYTHM	W—FOOT PLACEMENT	DP
1	1 & 2	S	Fwd with RF (toe-out 1/8 L)	LO
2	3 & 4	S	Fwd with LF (pivot 1/8 L)	LO to CL
3	5	Q	Sd with RF	CL
4	6	Q	LF closes to RF (WC)	

FOLLOWING THE LEFT OPEN BASIC:

How steady you hold onto the dance position of your arms (your frame) *on your own*, meaning without pressing down on your partner's left shoulder or hanging from his own dance frame, is the key to your establishing a sense, a sort of communication system, that will alert you to what's in your partner's mind. This is especially true during any changes in dance positions that he might lead.

The heel of your left hand, neatly placed over your partner's left shoulder, is the hub of your partnering communication system. It is from where you first sense an oncoming movement, especially if he's mastered the all-important dance rule that *the body moves first*.

DANCE TIP:

With the exception of the Left Open Basic, every pattern in this chapter can be danced in as little space as that of half the parking space for a compact car. Often, a crowded dance floor offers you even less space than that. A good social dancer is not necessarily one who knows a lot of patterns but one who, like an experienced city driver, knows how to lead his partner through heavy traffic without ever having to blow the horn or overuse the break pedal.

Chapter 8

The Tango

Even among people who love to dance, the origin of some social dances is not common knowledge. But ask most anyone if they know where the tango comes from and most are likely to answer, "Argentina."

Since the early 1900s there have been various styles of tango and all credit their roots to a style of song popular in Argentina and Uruguay, the milonga, which some records indicate became a partner dance later on, around 1910.

The sound of the milonga is joyous, uplifting. It's been said that it was favored by the poor and working classes of Argentina, many of which had migrated to Buenos Aires from European countries around the end of the nineteenth century, looking for work and for a better life. Frustrated and disillusioned at not finding what they had expected, musicians and composers among them started to write lyrics to milonga melodies that told stories about the hopelessness of their lives.

At first, milonga songs were accompanied by guitar, violin and flute. Then, an accordion-like instrument similar to the concertina, the bandoneon, was added to the mix, eventually becoming the heart and soul of the tango and a main contributor of its subsequent evolution as a dance. But it was neither its melody nor its lyrics that made the

tango Argentina's signature song. That credit must be given to the greatest tango singer of all time, the Argentinian Carlos Gardel, whose brooding voice and musical phrasing expressed love, nostalgia, passion and frustration like no one had done before him or after his death in 1935.

Today, the style of tango that most resembles the original milonga is the Argentinian tango, a dance consisting of complex patterns during which partners hold their bodies in a tight embrace, and where their feet and thighs seem to weave, slither and coil around each other like snakes.

In the early twenties, the tango became the new dance rage of Paris much of it thanks to the popularity of the American dance team, Irene and Vernon Castle. Before the Castles' time, dances were made up of long sequences of choreographed movements. Vernon Castle was the first dancer to break these sequences into what he called "figures" which he then taught at their New York City dance studio.

Like so many social dances, the tango has a long history of up-and-down swings in popularity. Starting around the mid-1980s, the Argentinian tango has continued an upswing in popularity among ballroom dancers much of it credited to the success of touring stage shows like Tango Argentino and Forever Tango. However, the style and patterns of the tangos featured in stage shows are highly choreo-graphed. As flashy and entertaining as they are, they're far from what you'd see anyone dancing at a social event.

Today, there are two predominant styles of ball-room tango, the International (English) tango and the American tango. Both are offshoots of the Argentinian tango. However, unlike their predecessor, they're both characterized by forward-and-back walking steps danced with a heel lead, and by a cat-like leg action where the feet move slightly ahead of the body in patterns that move across the floor as well as on the line of dance.

Unlike the foxtrot, where we aim to shift (roll) the body's weight smoothly from step to step, both the American tango and, more so, the International tango give their patterns a staccato look and feel. This is accomplished by a step-and-hold mode where dancers seem to rush toward the downbeat counts "1" and "3," holding their upright position still on upbeats "2" and "4," rushing counts "5" and "6" and then dragging the moving foot toward the supporting foot on counts "7" and "8" without shift-ing weight. This last three-steps, four counts, move is known as the "tango close." It is a short pattern that's as characteristic of tango dancing, including its often overused head snap, as is the rise-and-fall of the waltz.

Of the two styles, the American style is the least strict in terms of techniques and the least complex in terms of the overall structure of its patterns. It is therefore the style widely considered to be the most social of the two. Today, however, many American style tango dancers have incorporated into the style modified adaptations of many of the more staccato and flashier moves of the International style.

Some describe the tango as a dramatic dance. Others describe it as a dance of passion. To me the tango is all that and more. It is a display of various emotions—passion, conflict, strength, romance, po-wer, submission, empowerment—brought out by the steady heartbeat of a pulsating melody and being exchanged by two people, a male partner who leads the way and a female partner who lights up the path.

While there's a minimal chance that tangos will be played at any party or wedding you'll attend, you can certainly have a lot of fun learning and practicing some of the basic patterns that follow.

Fundamental Elements of the Tango

FOOTWORK

In the American style tango all forward steps are taken with a heel lead and with the weight of the body quickly shifting onto the entire foot. Side steps are taken with either the inside edge of the foot, with the weight quickly shifting onto the entire foot, or they are taken on the whole foot. On back steps we step on the ball of the feet.

TIMING AND RHYTHM

Tango dance music is written in 4/4 timing—four beats to a measure of music. Some tangos are also composed in 2/4 and 6/8 timing.

The rhythm of tango dance patterns varies between combinations of SQQ (4 counts) and SSQQS (8 beats). In some tango patterns forward, back and side steps are also danced to a single count, a Quick rhythm (QQS). The best tango dance tempo ranges between 30 and 32 MPM (measures per minute).

DANCE STANCE, FRAMES, POSITIONS, AND HOLDS

In the tango, dancers maintain the same upright postural stance characteristic of smooth dances. However, the knees are kept at a slightly bent angle throughout the dance.

Generally, tango dance patterns start and end in CL Dance Position. But changes of dance position within a dance pattern happen frequently, especially in more advanced dance patterns.

Closed Dance Position

There's a slight difference between the CL Dance Position of the tango and that of the foxtrot or the waltz. Because of the dance's characteristic quick moves staccato style, partners sit lower on bent knees, and the man generally places his partner a little farther off to his right than in the foxtrot or the waltz.

Left Open Dance Position

In the tango, the LO Dance Position is a transitional position. Meaning, partners start a dance pattern in CL, then they open up into LO for just a couple of individual steps and quickly return to CL. Many female dancers stylize the LO Position by arching their back and keeping the right side of their body long and looking strong.

Tango portrays a look of strength and defiance.

Partners moving in LO Position.

Dance Pattern Building Blocks

Tango dance patterns consist of forward and back walking steps, of side steps during which the feet close but never change weight, and of rocking steps.

The Tango Walk

Many tangos were first composed as marches, such as "La Cumparsita," one of the oldest and still most identifiable tango melodies. This melody was also one of the first tango melodies to include drums in its orchestration. Hence, the reason why many describe the look of forward and back tango steps as a sort of marching step. My favorite way to describe a tango walk is "visualize how a hunting cat or tiger approach its prey." The knees bend and straighten. The body sits low. The front legs seem to move in slow motion, pausing slightly at the completion of every step. Then, suddenly, the whole body springs for the kill.

The Tango Close

This characteristic three-step movement is identical to the foxtrot's Forward Half Box Step, with two exceptions: It is danced to a QQS rhythm, rather than a SQQ rhythm.

And it features a hesitation-like, sideward, movement of the traveling foot, commonly referred to as "a drag." Although the entire, three-movement sequence is called a tango close, the dragging foot never quite closes to the supporting foot. It stays slightly to the side of it free of any weight and ready to take the next step.

Once you learn the "tango close" just about any other steps you take before it or after it is a walking step, a rocking step or a combination of the two. Let's start by learning the tango close before we proceed further.

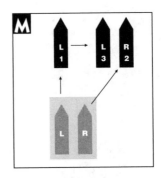
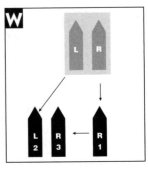

TIMING: 4/4
RHYTHM: QQS
NUMBER OF COUNTS: 4
NUMBER OF STEPS: 3 plus a hesitation "drag" step

Step	Count	Rhythm	M—Foot Placement	W—Foot Placement	DP
1	1	Q	Fwd with LF	Bk with RF	CL
2	2	Q	Sd with RF	Sd with LF	
3	3 & 4	S	Drag LF to RF (NWC)	Drag RF to LF (NWC)	

Step 1 of tango close.

Step 2 of tango close.

The Drag Move. Step 3 of tango close.

Contra Body Motion (CBM)

Contra Body Motion refers to the movement of the upper body (the torso) in opposition to the moving foot. For example, if the left foot is about to move forward into a turn, or about to move forward before the man is to lead his partner into a turn, the right side of the body is turned toward the left foot: CBM (Left). If it is the right foot that's to perform those movements, it is then the left side of the body that the man turns toward his right foot: CBM (Right).

CHARACTERISTIC STYLE OF THE TANGO

If you've seen movie or television programs featuring tango dancing, then you already know that the tango can be a very flashy and showy dance. For your own fun and enjoyment I've added some flashy options to the patterns featured in this chapter. However, I leave

it to your own discretion whether you'd want to try them out at a party. That is, unless you don't mind clearing the dance floor and having everyone stand around watching you and your partner.

Characteristically, the tango is a dance of stop-and-go types of movements. We refer to them as staccato. In the tango the constantly bent position of the knees and the quick movements of the torso and shoulders, all while maintaining a firm and steady dance frame, call for a great deal of balance and strength. This is one smooth dance that doesn't look good unless partners maintain very close body contact. Thus, it is a dance I don't recommend anyone trying out in public with someone they've never danced with before.

About Performing Tango Rocking Steps

In a tango, a rocking move is slightly different than it is in the waltz or the foxtrot where a rocking move is called "a balance." Meaning, in those two dances, you end up shifting your body's entire weight onto the forward and the back foot, respectively.

Conversely, in a tango rock, the body's weight stays balanced in between the forward and the back step. Although the body does rock, and the respective feet do come off the floor a bit, the body's weight is never quite shifted in whole to either forward or back foot, especially because the rocking moves are each performed to one single count (Q).

The second step of a rock step is described as In Place (In-Pl). This means that the rocking foot comes off its placement only to step right back onto the same spot on the count that follows. For example, A rock back in-place onto RF, means that the RF has been lifted from the dance floor then returned to the same spot on the next step.

Leading and Following the Rock and Corté Lunge

Men: In order to lead the Corté Lunge, you must prepare the move on the step prior to the actual lunge, Step 3, by bending your right knee and immediately moving your left leg back into a longer than usual step. That will tell your partner that she needs to respond with a longer forward step, her own Corté Lunge. Then, as your weight settles on that step, bend the knee into a lunge position. It also helps for you to apply CBM on Step 1. Then, as you step back on Step 3, also bring your left shoulder back. Leading back with the shoulder will result in your left knee, leg and foot (the lunging foot) turning outwards and providing you with a wider base on which to rest your upper body.

Women: As you head into the forward Corté Lunge, let the right side of your body lead the way. This will help you keep a firmer balance over the lunging leg. By letting the right side of your body be in line with the right lunging leg, you will also be able to arch your back with more ease and grace.

Partners dancing a forward rock with CBM.

A basic Rock and Corté Lunge.

A stylized Rock and Corté Lunge.

Tango Dance Pattern No. 1

The Tango Basic A

TIMING: 4/4
RHYTHM: SSQQS
NUMBER OF COUNTS: 8
NUMBER OF STEPS: 5
CHARACTERISTICS: This is the tango's signature pattern. It consists of two walking steps followed by the unique tango Close Ending.

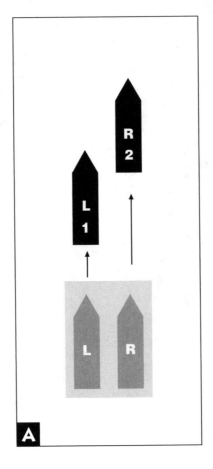

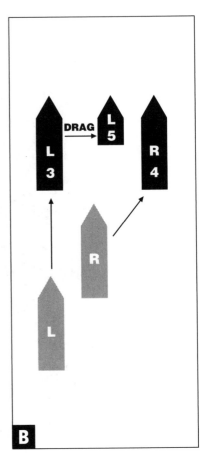

Box	Step	Count	Rhythm	M—Foot Placement	DP
A	1	1 & 2	S	Fwd with LF	CL
	2	3 & 4	S	Fwd with RF	
B	3	5	Q	Fwd with LF	
	4	6	Q	Sd with RF	
	5	7 & 8	S	Drag LF to RF (NWC)	

Tango Dance Pattern No. 1

The Tango Basic A

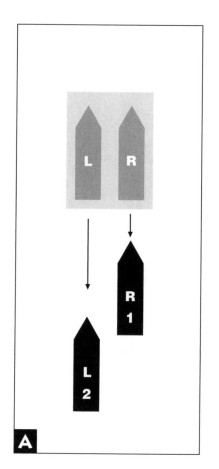

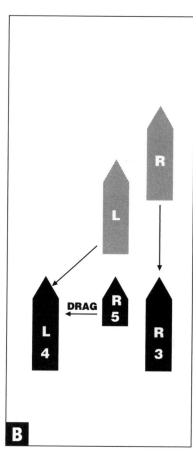

TIMING: 4/4
RHYTHM: SSQQS
NUMBER OF COUNTS: 8
NUMBER OF STEPS: 5
CHARACTERISTICS: This is the tango's signature pattern. It consists of two walking steps followed by the unique tango Close Ending.

Box	Step	Count	Rhythm	W—Foot Placement	DP
A	1	1 & 2	S	Bk with RF	CL
	2	3 & 4	S	Bk with LF	
B	3	5	Q	Bk with RF	
	4	6	Q	Sd with LF	
	5	7 & 8	S	Drag RF to LF (NWC)	

Tango Dance Pattern No. 2

The Tango Basic B (Left Open)

TIMING: 4/4

RHYTHM: SSQQS

NUMBER OF COUNTS: 8

NUMBER OF STEPS: 5

CHARACTERISTICS: This pattern starts from CL Dance Position, opening into LO Dance Position on the first step. On the second step, the man leads his partner to pivot to her left to end up facing him in CL Dance Position.

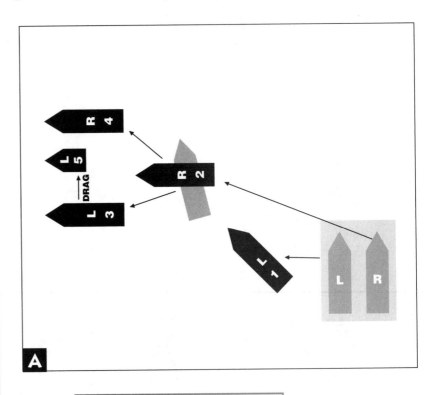

DANCE TIP:

LEADING THE LEFT OPEN BASIC

The lead for this dance pattern is all done by the man's shoulders and dance frame. As he's about to take his second step, he must turn his torso a quarter turn to his left in order to (1) lead his partner into a pivot turn and (2) place her back into CL Dance Position.

DVD LESSON:

Your tango DVD chapter includes a segment that breaks down the two previous patterns and then links them.

Box	Step	Count	Rhythm	M—Foot Placement	DP
A	1	1 & 2	S	Fwd with LF (toe-in 1/8 Trn L)	LO
	2	3 & 4	S	Fwd and across RF	CL
	3	5	Q	Fwd with LF	
	4	6	Q	Sd with RF	
	5	7 & 8	S	Drag LF to RF (NWC)	

Tango Dance Pattern No. 2

W

The Tango Basic B (Left Open)

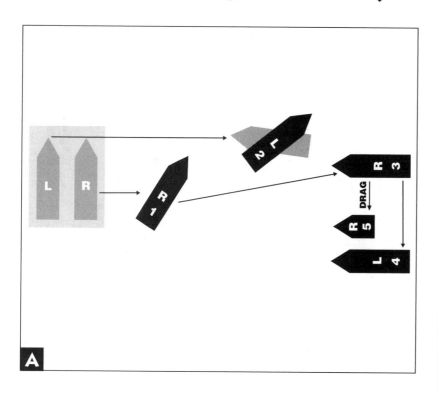

TIMING: 4/4
RHYTHM: SSQQS
NUMBER OF COUNTS: 8
NUMBER OF STEPS: 5
CHARACTERISTICS: This pattern starts from CL Dance Position, opening into LO Dance Position on the first step. On the second step, the man leads his partner to pivot to her left to end up facing him in CL Dance Position.

DVD LESSON:

Your tango DVD chapter includes a segment that breaks down the two previous patterns and then links them.

BOX	STEP	COUNT	RHYTHM	W—FOOT PLACEMENT	DP
A	1	1 & 2	S	Fwd with RF (toe-out 1/8 Trn R)	LO
	2	3 & 4	S	Fwd with LF (pivot 1/2 to L)	CL
	3	5	Q	Bk with RF	
	4	6	Q	Sd with LF	
	5	7 & 8	S	Drag RF to LF (NWC)	

Tango Dance Pattern No. 3

Rock and Corté Lunge

TIMING: 4/4

RHYTHM: QQS S QQS

NUMBER OF COUNTS: 10

NUMBER OF STEPS: 7

CHARACTERISTICS: This pattern combines a left and right foot rock with a back lunge (forward for the woman). The lunge can be held for an extra count for more dramatic value or it can danced into and then immediately out of it. During the actual lunge, the man maintains his upright posture, but his partner can add a lot of flair to the pattern by arching her back away from her partner.

DVD LESSON:

Your DVD tango chapter includes a segment that features this pattern and links it with the previous ones.

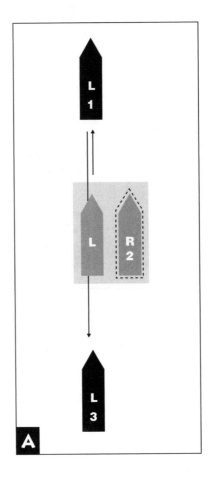

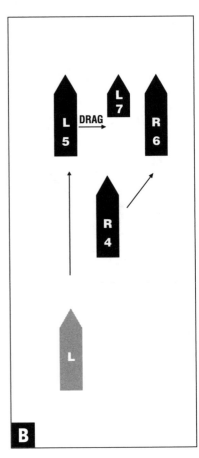

Box	Step	Count	Rhythm	M—Foot Placement	DP
A	1	1	Q	Rock Fwd with LF (CBM)	CL
	2	2	Q	Bk In-Pl with RF	
	3	3 & 4	S	Bk with LF (Lunge)	
B	4	5 & 6	S	Fwd with RF	
	5	7	Q	Fwd with LF	
	6	8	Q	Sd with RF	
	7	9 & 10	S	Drag LF to RF (NWC)	

Tango Dance Pattern No. 3

W

Rock and Corté Lunge

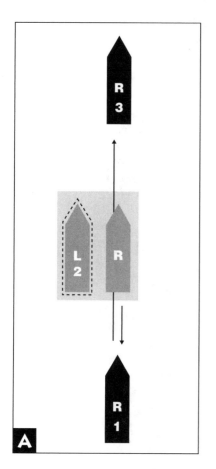

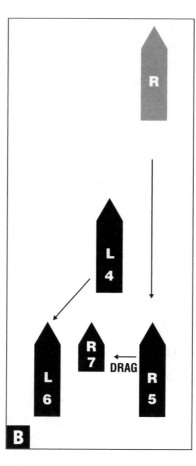

TIMING: 4/4
RHYTHM: QQS S QQS
NUMBER OF COUNTS: 10
NUMBER OF STEPS: 7
CHARACTERISTICS: This pattern combines a left and right foot rock with a back lunge (forward for the woman). The lunge can be held for an extra count for more dramatic value or it can danced into and then immediately out of it. During the actual lunge, the man maintains his upright posture, but his partner can add a lot of flair to the pattern by arching her back away from her partner.

DVD LESSON:

Your DVD tango chapter includes a segment that features this pattern and links it with the previous ones.

Box	Step	Count	Rhythm	W—Foot Placement	DP
A	1	1	Q	Rock Bk with RF (CBM)	CL
	2	2	Q	Fwd In-Pl with LF	
	3	3 & 4	S	Fwd with RF (Lunge)	
B	4	5 & 6	S	Bk with LF	
	5	7	Q	Bk with RF	
	6	8	Q	Sd with LF	
	7	9 & 10	S	Drag RF to LF (NWC)	

Part Three

The Latin Rhythm Dances

Latin dances come from various Caribbean islands and South American countries. Before the turn of the nineteenth century, these countries had been under Spanish, French, or Portuguese domination, and their trade of slaves from Africa into the Americas was widespread. With them, slaves brought native dances and percussion musical instruments that were eventually integrated into the music and dances of the colonial cultures. That integration paved the way for the Latin rhythms and dances that we know today.

The rumba, the mambo, and the cha-cha evolved from another dance, the son, an offshoot of the danzón, Cuba's national dance since 1922. But the danzón, a slow tempo rumba/bolero with a steadily pulsating 4/4 beat structure was in itself an offshoot of the habanera, a dance of colonial times which evolved from the contradanza, a dance of French origin that came to Cuba via slaves from Haiti.

To enthusiasts of traditional ballroom dancing, Latin dances like the mambo, the rumba, the bolero, the cha-cha, the samba and the merengue have been popular since the 1930s. Since the early 1990s, however, another Latin dance, the salsa, a more contemporary version of the mambo, has become the most popular Latin dance. Like the mambo, salsa is a style of music as well as of dance. Unlike its predecessor, salsa's origin must be credited to the work of musicians like the late Tito Puente, and the legendary Celia Cruz.

Like the music and dance of their Afro-Cuban and Afro-Creole roots, Latin dances are characterized by percussive sounds and compact sequences of short steps, which allow for isolated body movements that are further accented by the Cuban hip motion. Latin dances feature a variety of open dance positions and dance holds which change often. Movements like underarm turns, pivots, swivels and solo spins make Latin dances fun to learn and to do. They also allow for a lot of individual expression.

In the following chapters you will find that many of the fundamental elements of each of the Latin dances I include in this book are equally shared by most of them. As a result, you will find a certain amount of the same textual descriptions repeated a couple of times—Cuban motion, footwork, etc. Although repetition is key to learning and memorizing dance patterns and their related technical elements, you may want to skip those segments if you feel comfortable with them.

Chapter 9

The Rumba

When I was a kid, I used to marvel at how great my parents looked when dancing a danzón not knowing that, even back then, people referred to it as the dance of the "old folks" because of its simple signature pattern: a side-to-side rocking step each capped with a slight hip lift during which couples seldom moved from the same spot. The precursor to the danzón was the son, another "spot dance" considered to be the mother of Cuban dances like the rumba which came after it. The mambo followed the rumba. The cha-cha was the last of the Latin dances to have become popular in the U.S. during the mid-fifties.

The rumba is both a dance and a style of music that bears several names. The original Cuban rumba has a fast tempo that's more associated with Afro-Cuban movements like the guaracha and the guagancó. For the ballroom style rumba there are three basic tempos.

The slowest tempo rumba (27-28 MPM) is called the bolero. It resembles the danzón in that its basic dance pattern is an Open Box Step which starts with dancers stepping to the side followed by a back break for the man and a forward break for the woman.

The medium tempo rumba (30-32 MPM) is the one most often played and danced. It is also the one that lends itself to the American ballroom style of dance for which the Closed Box Step is the signature pattern.

The International style rumba varies in tempo between 32 and 34 MPM. Its signature pattern is an open box step much like the danzón. It differs from the American-style rumba in the choreographic structure of signature dance patterns, of footwork, and of weight-shifting hip action. It is also one of the showiest and sexiest dances of that style's competition dance curriculum.

Also, the rumba brings together all the fundamental elements of Latin dances in general—footwork, dance positions, dance stand, hip motion. By learning them you will be able to breeze through the salsa, the cha-cha, and the merengue.

Fundamental Elements of the Rumba

FOOTWORK (FT)

The footwork for the rumba follows the standard rule of Latin Dances Characteristic Footwork:

On forward and back steps, it is the balls of the feet that are first to be placed on the dance floor.

But as the body's weight is fully shifted from the weight-supporting foot onto the new step, the foot flattens. This is why the footwork of the rumba, and of all Latin dances, is referred to as ball-flat.

Forward and back steps are to be taken on the balls of the feet.

The foot flattens as the body's weight is shifted onto it.

When stepping off to the side, it is the inside edge of the ball of the moving foot that's first placed on the dance floor.

Then, the entire foot presses down on the dance floor as it receives the full weight of the body.

Side steps are small steps taken with the inside edge of the feet.

As it receives the full weight of the body, the foot flattens and the knee straightens.

Relation Between Footwork and Weight Shifting Action

The shifting of body weight from one weight-bearing step (or supporting foot) onto the next weight-bearing step (or moving foot), involves a mechanical chain reaction that starts with the feet and ends with the hips.

One quick way to feel and understand the mechanics involved during this weight-shifting action is to climb up a couple of steps of a flight of stairs. As you take the first step, the ball of the foot is placed down first. Its corresponding knee is in a bent position. Your body then leans forward over the thigh of the bent knee to climb the step, exerting downward pressure on the ankle and entire foot. The downward pressure of the body's weight causes the knee to straighten as you finally climb that one step.

When stepping to the side, we shift the weight by first placing (or "pressing down" onto the dance floor) the inside edge of the moving foot. Then, as the full weight of the body is transferred onto the pressing foot, its corresponding knee straightens and the body is back standing tall. But as we take the next step, the hip of the straightened leg shifts farther outwards and the entire process starts all over again.

When stepping back, the weight-shifting process is almost identical to that which takes place as we step forward, but in reverse and not with as much of a hip action. The motion interaction that takes place between the correct foot placement, the bending and straightening of the knees and, ultimately, the shift of weight from the supporting foot to the moving foot results in a hip action we often refer to as "Cuban motion."

TIMING AND RHYTHM

Latin music is written in groups (measures) of four beats (counts): 4/4. Most social level rumba dance patterns take four to eight measures to complete and consist of sequences of individual steps that are taken in rhythmic combinations of one count of music per individual step (a Quick rhythm) and two counts of music per individual step (a Slow rhythm), making the characteristic rhythm pattern of the rumba a QQS.

However, I must also note that some dance instructors teach the rumba with partners taking their first step forward (or back for women) instead of to the side. In this case, the characteristic rhythm becomes SQQ, altering the more widely accepted rhythmic breakdown of the original ballroom-style Cuban rumba, but not its signature patterns.

DANCE STANCE, FRAME, POSITIONS, AND HOLDS

Unlike smooth dances, Latin dances are all about isolated, rhythmically expressive movements of the shoulders, rib cage, hips and knees. A dancer's stance is therefore not as upright and poised as it is in smooth dances. Instead, Latin dancers maintain a forward-leaning stance and a more relaxed dance frame with arms staying closer to the sides of their bodies.

In many rumba dance patterns, dancers break the traditional Closed Dance Position frame, especially during patterns that include underarm turns, cross body leads, and spins.

The Latin Dance relaxed frame.

Rumba dance partners in CL Dance Position.

Closed Dance Position (CL)

There is no body contact between partners.

They stand facing each other about one foot apart and holding their arms in a more relaxed dance frame.

The woman's left hand is placed on the side of the man's right arm, just below the shoulder joint. The palm of her right hand is in contact with the palm of the man's left hand with the fingers loosely closed over the outer edge of the man's left index finger.

The man's right hand is held under the woman's left shoulder blade. His fingers should stay close, but men lead with the outer edge of the right hand not with the fingers. (Little bothers a woman as much as feeling her partner's fingers digging into her back.) The man's left hand is held off to the side at about chest

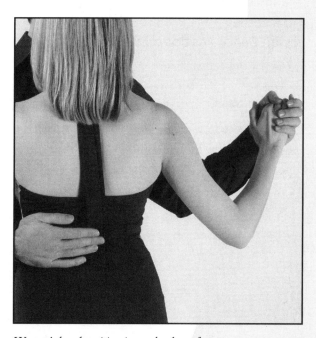

Woman's hand position in rumba dance frame.

level and with the elbow bent. The man's left hand is a place where his partner rests her hand. It is not what the man uses to grab or hold onto his partner.

Just as partners may change dance positions within a dance pattern, they often also change dance holds. The dance holds of the patterns featured in this chapter include the Open Dance Position with a One-Hand Hold and a Two-Hand Hold.

Man's hand position in rumba dance frame.

Open Dance Position–One-Hand Hold (1HH)

Partners stand farther apart with the palm of the woman's right hand resting on the palm of the man's left hand. The free hands can be held in a variety of positions, but the most common is off to the side for the woman and off to the side or next to the body with the elbow bent for the man.

Open Dance Position–One-Hand Hold (1HH).

Open Dance Position–Two-Hand Hold (2HH)

Partners are holding each other with opposite hands.

Open dance position—Two-Hand Hold (2HH).

DANCE PATTERN BUILDING BLOCKS

Rumba dance patterns consist of forward, back or side, single walking steps combined with forward, back or side rock/break steps.

Rocking Steps Forward, Back and Side

In dance terminology, rocking steps are called "break" steps because, just like when bringing a car into a full stop, a break step is the first and last step given in one specific direction. For instance, if you were standing still and took one single step to your right with your right foot then immediately

retrieved that step and brought it right back to its place of origin, you would be dancing a "side break." Here are diagrams of these breaks. You can practically dance them by just moving your feet while sitting down.

Forward and Back Breaks:

STEP	M & W—FOOT PLACEMENT
1	Fwd with LF
2	Bk In-Pl* with RF
3	LF to RF (WC)
4	Bk with RF
5	Fwd In-Pl with LF
6	RF to LF (WC)

Side-to-Side Breaks:

STEP	M & W—FOOT PLACEMENT
1	Sd with LF
2	Sd In-Pl* with RF
3	Close LF to RF (WC)
4	Sd with RF
5	Sd In-Pl with LF
6	Close RF to LF (WC)

*In-Pl: This is an abbreviation for "in place," one that you will find quite often when describing rock/break foot placements. In-Pl means that you have taken your foot off the dance floor and then placed it back in the same place.

Fifth Position Break:

Back breaks during which the breaking foot is placed behind the supporting foot with its toe pointing outwards is commonly referred to as a "Fifth" Position Break. Another name for it is also a "whisk." You can also try out this one while sitting down.

STEP	M & W—FOOT PLACEMENT
1	Cross the LF behind the RF
2	Step Fwd In-Pl* with the RF (WC)
3	Step Sd with LF
4	Cross the RF behind the LF
5	Step Fwd In-Pl with the LF (WC)

*In Place.

Position of feet in Fifth Position Break Steps.

Latin Walking Steps

A Latin walk is one that is performed with Latin footwork and hip motion traveling forward or backward. Generally, a Latin walk is one single step that links two break steps.

In Latin walks, hips move in opposition to the traveling foot.

The Closed Box Step

The Closed Box Step is the rumba's signature pattern. It consists of two groups of three steps each. In the first group, the forward half of the box, the feet move side and forward. In the second group, the back half of the box, they move side and back. The woman usually performs the back half first in order to mirror the man's steps. This pattern is very similar to the box steps of the waltz and tango except that you start by moving to the side rather than to the front.

Forward Half of a Box Step:

Step	Count	Rhythm	M & W—Foot Placement
1	1	Q	Sd with LF
2	2	Q	Close RF to LF (WC)
3	3	S	Fwd with LF

Back Half of a Box Step:

Step	Count	Rhythm	M & W—Foot Placement
4	4	Q	Sd with RF
5	5	Q	Close LF to RF (WC)
6	6	S	Bk with RF

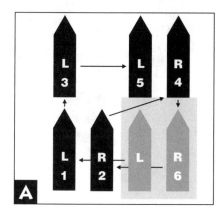

Pivot and Spin Movements

A pivot is a swivel-turn that is executed over the weight-supporting foot. The turning degree of a pivot ranges between 1/8 of a turn to 1/2 of a turn. A spin is a turn during which the body rotates 3/4 to 1 full turn or more on one weight-bearing foot. Most turns that a man would lead his partner into will call for her to perform either a pivot or a spin.

The Cross Body Lead

The Cross Body Lead is a dance pattern as well as a dance move. In both roles it is one of the most danced in the overall curriculum of Latin dances, especially those that evolved from the rumba. It is the dance pattern most often performed as a lead-in for a wide range of turns and spins and for linking together segments of other dance patterns. In fact, without learning and mastering the Cross Body Lead you really can't say you know how to dance a rumba, or a cha-cha, or a mambo or a salsa. A cross body lead can be danced in various dance positions.

The three words that make up the name of this pattern can be taken as a simple description of it: After completing a full box step in CL Dance Position, the man lowers his left hand hold as he turns to the left moving away from his partner and thus breaking their CL Dance Position. He then leads her to step forward across the front line of his body. Following that step, he then leads her to pivot to her left on her left foot. From this step, he can either move forward into a half box or he can continue leading his partner into a variety of left turns and spins.

Cross body lead in CL Dance Position.

Cross body lead in Open 1HH Position.

CHARACTERISTIC STYLING OF THE RUMBA

Cuban Hip Motion

In the rumba, the action of the hips (Cuban motion) is a constant one, although it appears to be emphasized more on forward and back steps than on side steps because forward and back steps are generally danced to two counts of music, a Slow rhythm step.

Cuban hip motion is not solely the work of the hips. It is the end result of a sequence of coordinated movements that involve the feet, ankles and knees. Once that coordination is mastered, dance instructors will start teaching their students an additional movement that also involves the rib cage.

The simplest way I have found for beginners to get their feet, knees and hips working together and, ultimately, get their entire body moving with an authentic Latin dance rhythmic look is through the following exercise. Please, try it often. I always made my students start their lessons with it.

Follow the instructions written for each photograph as if you were standing in front of a mirror, i.e., the models' left hip is your right hip and your left leg is their right leg.

1.   Start with feet apart and the body's weight equally distributed (50/50) between both feet, keeping both knees slightly bent.

Starting position.

2. Shift the right hip over to the right leg, letting the leg straighten as the hip settles over it.

3. Now, shift the left hip over to the left leg, letting that leg straighten as the hip settles over it.

Hip shifts sideways over weight-supporting leg.

Hip shifts in opposite direction as weight shifts again.

4. Try doing this several times. At every try, see if you can keep your upper body as much in-between both feet as possible. By the way, the only way you are going to accomplish that is by keeping your rib cage from moving over to either side, thus isolating your hips from the rest of the upper body.

Now let's go a couple of steps further.

1. Start with your feet apart and your body's weight equally distributed (50/50) between both feet, keeping both knees slightly bent.

2. Shift the right hip over to the right leg again. However, this time, as your right hip settles over the straightened right leg, let the knee of the left leg draw the left foot over to the right foot. It should feel as if the right hip's settling action is what ultimately draws the moving foot toward the supporting foot.

3. Now, let the left side of your upper body (the rib cage) lean sideways toward the left foot, applying some pressure on that foot. Then, place the entire foot on the floor while you shift your right hip over to it, freeing the right foot of the body's weight.

Rib cage and knee/hip relation on weight shifting movement.

Knee/hip relation on weight shifting movement.

Try repeating the above exercise by performing four to six continuous side steps, paying attention to how the feet, the knees and the hips interact during the shift of weight. Before you know it, you will be moving the Latin way.

DVD LESSON:

Your DVD includes a how-to Cuban motion chapter.

The 50/50 Rule of Latin Dance Lead and Follow

That the man leads and the woman follows is a rather misguiding statement because it makes it sound as if all the responsibility of good partnering rests on men. Nothing can be farther from the truth. Without an equal share, a 50/50 communication system between partners, one or both will find themselves pushing or pulling the other. That may be acceptable in mud wrestling, but not in partner dancing.

The 50/50 partnering communication in the Rumba does change according to the dance position of the partners. However, the key to it is found on whether both dancers are initiating upcoming changes in dance positions, dance patterns or individual moves through actions involving their entire body or not. Meaning, in all styles of partner dancing, THE BODY MOVES FIRST–THE DANCE FRAME MOVES SECOND–THE FEET MOVE THIRD–all within either a full beat of music or even a fraction of a beat of music.

In Closed Dance Position, it is via her left hand that the woman should first get a sense of the direction toward which her partner is about to move. Simultaneously, it is the man's left and right hands (the communication endpoints of his dance frame) that must follow the intended movement of his upper body in order for his partner to follow suit with hers.

In all Open Positions, the 50/50 relationship is mostly left to the wrists and fingers. The fingers of the woman's right or left hand always face down and are placed over the fingers of the man's right or left hand which always face upwards, connecting into a hinge-like position. This hold is often referred to as "palm-to-palm."

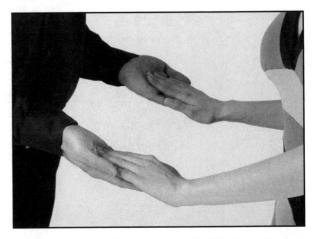

Palm-to-palm is the characteristic hand hold in Open Dance Positions.

Partners seldom stand or dance at full arm's length. Instead, they keep the elbows bent at a comfortable angle and according to their heights. The man always adjusts the level at which he keeps his frame to the height of his partner.

If Walls Could Talk

Here is a simple exercise that will help you feel and understand how the body, the wrists, elbows and forearms interact to communicate a dance lead and to sense a dance lead.

1. Face a wall and step back away from it at arm's length.
2. Place the fingertips of both hands on the wall at about waist level.
3. Bend your knees, slightly.
4. Lean forward from the waist, letting your elbows and wrist feel some of the body's forward leaning pressure.

5. Keeping your elbows pointing down and at equal distance from each other, bend your right knee directly over the front of your right foot. At the same time, let your right shoulder and right side of your rib cage move closer to the wall. You should feel your weight shifting more over to your right side. You should also feel more pressure being exerted on your wrists and fingers as you move closer to the wall.

In underarm turns, women continue to press fingers against the palm of man's hands.

That's the sort of communication I'm talking about. If the wall could talk, it would tell you that it feels the right side of your body coming closer to it and the left side of the body backing away.

If you were doing this exercise with a friend or dance partner, and you should, you should do it with your eyes shut close. You would then sense each other's movement and shift of weight, as long as both of you kept that even, light forward pressure on your wrists.

When you are in a One- or Two-Hand Hold, feeling that 50/50 degree of communication is a lot easier. It is when you're leading or following a turn, especially an underarm turn, that it is tougher to maintain that bilateral firmness.

In such cases, it is the woman's fingers that keep the lead-and-follow communication going by staying extended, but close, and pressing against the palm of the man's open hand.

In underarm turns, the man's open left hand acts as a wall of support for his partner. It's almost as if, once she senses the lead, she pushes herself away from the hand into the turn only to find the hand again for support when she completes the turn.

Now, let's rumba!

Rumba Dance Pattern No. 1

The Closed Box Step

TIMING: 4/4
RHYTHM: QQS
NUMBER OF COUNTS: 8
NUMBER OF ACTUAL STEPS: 6
CHARACTERISTICS: Short steps with weight changing (WC) from moving foot to supporting foot every time feet come together.

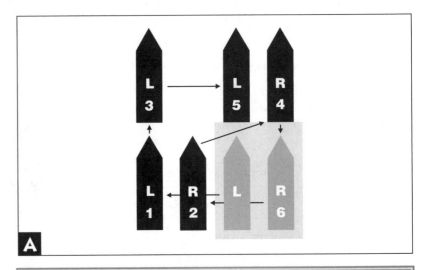

Box	Step	Count	Rhythm	M—Foot Placement	DP
A	1	1	Q	Sd with LF	CL
	2	2	Q	Close RF to LF (WC)	
	3	3 & 4	S	Fwd with LF	
	4	5	Q	Sd with RF	
	5	6	Q	Close LF to RF (WC)	
	6	7 & 8	S	Bk with RF	

The Closed Box Step, the signature pattern of the American style rumba, consists of two sets of three steps: two side steps, where the body's weight changes on the second step as the moving foot closes next to the supporting foot, and one forward or back step. When the side steps are followed by a forward step, you're dancing the Forward Half of the Box Step. When the side steps are followed by a back step, you're dancing the Back Half of the Box Step.

Either of the two halves is the usual lead-in move to many rumba patterns. Likewise, most patterns end with either of the two halves. As it is in all dances which have a Closed Box as a signature pattern, the woman's second half of the Box is identical to the man's first half. Meaning, the man's and woman's patterns are the mirror opposites of each other.

Rumba Dance Pattern No. 1

W

The Closed Box Step

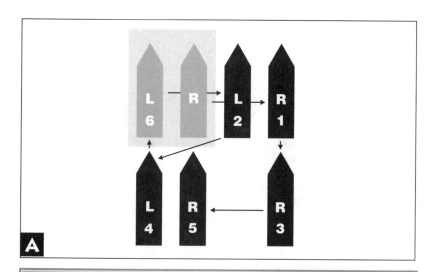

TIMING: 4/4
RHYTHM: QQS
NUMBER OF COUNTS: 8
NUMBER OF ACTUAL STEPS: 6
CHARACTERISTICS: Short steps with weight changing (WC) from moving foot to supporting foot every time feet come together.

Box	Step	Count	Rhythm	W—Foot Placement	DP
A	1	1	Q	Sd with RF	CL
	2	2	Q	Close LF to RF (WC)	
	3	3 & 4	S	Bk with RF	
	4	5	Q	Sd with LF	
	5	6	Q	Close RF to LF (WC)	
	6	7 & 8	S	Fwd with LF	

Rumba Dance Pattern No. 2

The Turning Box Step

TIMING: 4/4
RHYTHM: QQS
NUMBER OF COUNTS: 8
NUMBER OF ACTUAL STEPS: 6
CHARACTERISTICS: All that distinguishes the Turning Box from the Closed Box is that 1/4 turns are danced on every forward and back step.

DANCE NOTE:

Once you have mastered the Turning Box, you will seldom want to dance it without turning.

A Closed Box Step can also be danced making gradual, 1/4 turns to the left. Each 1/4 turn is done on the forward and back steps to a Slow rhythm count (2 beats).

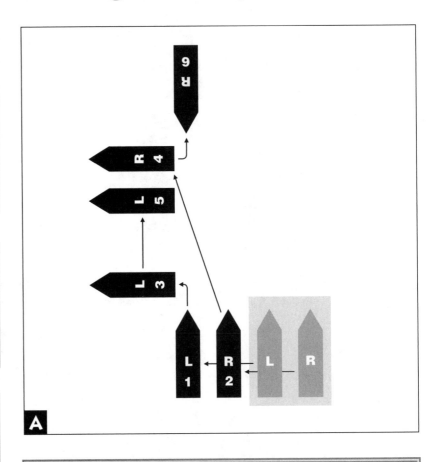

Box	Step	Count	Rhythm	M—Foot Placement	DP
A	1	1	Q	Sd with LF	CL
	2	2	Q	Close RF to LF (WC)	
	3	3 & 4	S	Fwd with LF (toe-out 1/4 Trn to L)	
	4	5	Q	Sd with RF	
	5	6	Q	Close LF to RF (WC)	
	6	7 & 8	S	Bk with RF (toe-in 1/4 Trn to L)	

Rumba Dance Pattern No. 2

W

The Turning Box Step

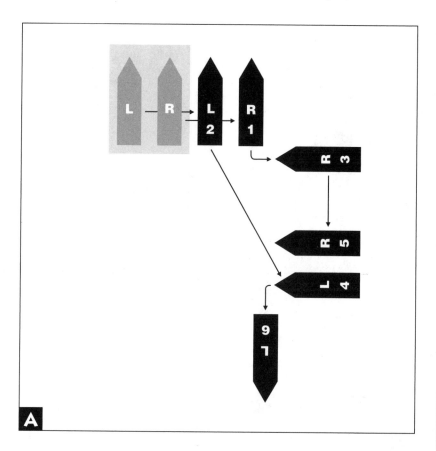

A

TIMING: 4/4
RHYTHM: QQS
NUMBER OF COUNTS: 8
NUMBER OF ACTUAL STEPS: 6
CHARACTERISTICS: All that distinguishes the Turning Box from the Closed Box is that 1/4 turns are danced on every forward and back step.

DANCE NOTE:

Once you have mastered the Turning Box, you will seldom want to dance it without turning.

A Closed Box Step can also be danced making gradual, 1/4 turns to the left. Each 1/4 turn is done on the forward and back steps to a Slow rhythm count (2 beats).

Box	Step	Count	Rhythm	W—Foot Placement	DP
A	1	1	Q	Sd with RF	CL
	2	2	Q	Close LF to RF (WC)	
	3	3 & 4	S	Bk with RF (toe-in 1/4 Trn to L)	
	4	5	Q	Sd with LF	
	5	6	Q	Close RF to LF (WC)	
	6	7 & 8	S	Fwd with LF (toe-out 1/4 Trn to L)	

Rumba Dance Pattern No. 3

The Fifth Position Breaks

TIMING: 4/4
RHYTHM: QQS
NUMBER OF COUNTS: 24
NUMBER OF ACTUAL STEPS: 18
CHARACTERISTICS: The Fifth Position Breaks start with the first three steps of a Box Turn followed by three side steps which then lead partners into the actual Fifth Position Rocking Break steps. During the breaks partners change dance positions from CL to LO and RO, changing dance holds every time.

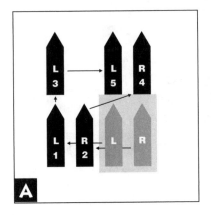

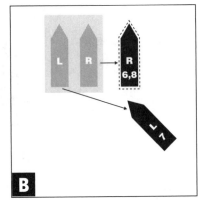

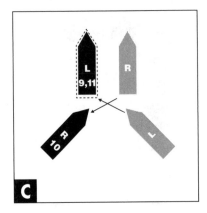

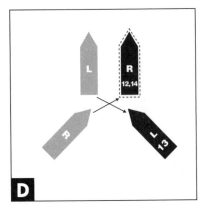

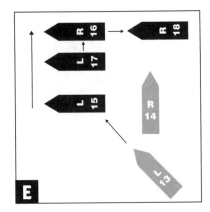

Rumba Dance Pattern No. 3

The Fifth Position Breaks

Box	Step	Count	Rhythm	M—Foot Placement	DP
A	1	1	Q	Sd with LF	CL
	2	2	Q	Close RF to LF (WC)	
	3	3 & 4	S	Fwd with LF	
	4	1	Q	Sd with RF	
	5	2	Q	Close LF to RF (WC)	
B	6	3 & 4	S	Sd with RF	
	7	1	Q	X LF behind RF	LO
	8	2	Q	Fwd In-Pl with RF	
C	9	3 & 4	S	Sd with LF	CL
	10	1	Q	X RF behind LF	RO
	11	2	Q	Fwd In-Pl with LF	
D	12	3 & 4	S	Sd with RF	CL
	13	1	Q	X LF behind RF	LO
	14	2	Q	Fwd In-Pl with RF	CL
E	15	3 & 4	S	Fwd with LF (1/4 Trn to L)	
	16	1	Q	Sd with RF	
	17	2	Q	Close LF to RF (WC)	
	18	3 & 4	S	Bk with RF	

This pattern takes its name from one of ballet dance's five positions of the feet. In a Fifth Position Break, one foot is placed with its toe pointing outwards and behind the supporting foot. In that position, partners then dance two rocking steps.

DVD LESSON:

Your DVD rumba chapter includes a segment featuring the Fifth Position Break, linking it with previous patterns and giving you some ideas for arm styling.

W

Rumba Dance Pattern No. 3

The Fifth Position Breaks

TIMING: 4/4

RHYTHM: QQS

NUMBER OF COUNTS: 24

NUMBER OF ACTUAL STEPS: 18

CHARACTERISTICS: The Fifth Position Breaks start with the first three steps of a Box Turn followed by three side steps which then lead partners into the actual Fifth Position Rocking Break steps. During the breaks partners change dance positions from CL to LO and RO, changing dance holds every time.

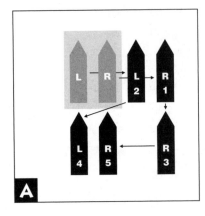

A

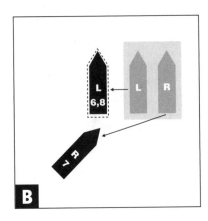

B

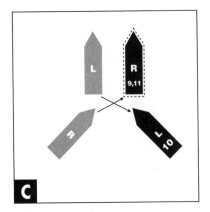

C

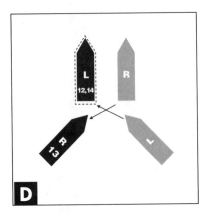

D

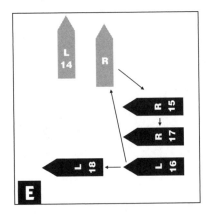

E

Rumba Dance Pattern No. 3

The Fifth Position Breaks

Box	Step	Count	Rhythm	W—Foot Placement	DP
A	1	1	Q	Sd with RF	CL
	2	2	Q	Close LF to RF (WC)	
	3	3 & 4	S	Bk with RF	
	4	1	Q	Sd with LF	
	5	2	Q	Close RF to LF (WC)	
B	6	3 & 4	S	Sd with LF	
	7	1	Q	X RF behind LF	LO
	8	2	Q	Fwd In-Pl with LF	
C	9	3 & 4	S	Sd with RF	CL
	10	1	Q	X LF behind RF	RO
	11	2	Q	Fwd In-Pl with RF	
D	12	3 & 4	S	Sd with LF	CL
	13	1	Q	X RF behind LF	LO
	14	2	Q	Fwd In-Pl with LF	CL
E	15	3 & 4	S	BK with RF (1/4 Trn to L)	
	16	1	Q	Sd with LF	
	17	2	Q	Close RF to LF (WC)	
	18	3 & 4	S	Fwd with LF	

This pattern takes its name from one of ballet dance's five positions of the feet. In a Fifth Position Break, one foot is placed with its toe pointing outwards and behind the supporting foot. In that position, partners then dance two rocking steps

DVD LESSON:

Your DVD rumba chapter includes a segment featuring the Fifth Position Break, linking it with previous patterns and giving you some ideas for arm styling.

Rumba Dance Pattern No. 4

The Underarm Turn

TIMING: 4/4
RHYTHM: QQS
NUMBER OF COUNTS: 16
NUMBER OF ACTUAL STEPS: 12
CHARACTERISTICS: For both the man and the woman this is a very simple pattern. He does nothing other than dance two full Box Steps (16 counts), raising his left arm after completing the first Box Step and leading his partner to turn under it to her right (a natural turn). After dancing a full Box Step, she's led into an Underarm Turn consisting of two forward walks, toward her partner's left side. She pivots 2 turns to the right, under his left hand, immediately followed by another pivot (3/4 turn to the right), ending up facing her partner.

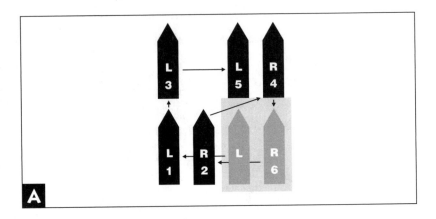

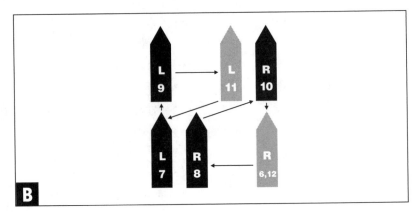

Rumba Dance Pattern No. 4

The Underarm Turn

M

Box	Step	Count	Rhythm	M—Foot Placement	DP
A	1	1	Q	Sd with LF	CL
	2	2	Q	Close RF to LF (WC)	
	3	3 & 4	S	Fwd with LF	
	4	1	Q	Sd with RF	
	5	2	Q	Close LF to RF (WC)	1HH
	6	3 & 4	S	Bk with RF	
B	7	1	Q	Sd with LF	
	8	2	Q	Close RF to LF (WC)	UA
	9	3 & 4	S	Fwd with LF	
	10	1	Q	Sd with RF	1HH
	11	2	Q	Close LF to RF (WC)	CL
	12	3 & 4	S	Bk with RF	

DVD LESSON:

Your DVD rumba chapters includes a segment featuring the Underarm Turn.

LEADING THE UNDERARM TURN

Steps 1–6 Dance a full Closed Box Step, releasing your right hand hold on step 6 and raising your left hand hold to indicate to your partner that she's to turn under your arm. You can also help guide her into the first step of the turn by placing your right hand on her back and guiding her through the first step of the turn.

Step 7 Raise your left hand to initiate the UA turn lead.

Step 8 As you step off to the side, start to lead the UA turn.

Step 9 Finish leading the turn.

Steps 10–12 Man dances the second half of his Closed Box Step, bringing partner back into CL Dance Position on step 12.

W

Rumba Dance Pattern No. 4

The Underarm Turn

TIMING: 4/4
RHYTHM: QQS
NUMBER OF COUNTS: 16
NUMBER OF ACTUAL STEPS: 12
CHARACTERISTICS: For both the man and the woman this is a very simple pattern. He does nothing other than dance two full Box Steps (16 counts), raising his left arm after completing the first Box Step and leading his partner to turn under it to her right (a natural turn). After dancing a full Box Step, she's led into an Underarm Turn consisting of two forward walks, toward her partner's left side. She pivots two turns to the right, under his left hand, immediately followed by another pivot (3/4 turn to the right), ending up facing her partner.

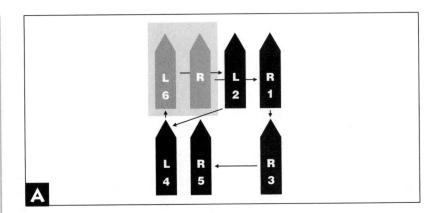

A

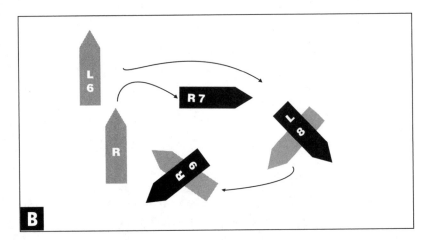

B

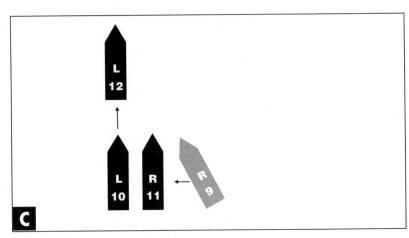

C

Rumba Dance Pattern No. 4

W

The Underarm Turn

Box	Step	Count	Rhythm	W—Foot Placement	DP
A	1	1	Q	Sd with RF	CL
	2	2	Q	Close LF to RF (WC)	
	3	3 & 4	S	Bk with RF	
	4	1	Q	Sd with LF	
	5	2	Q	Close RF to LF (WC)	1HH
	6	3 & 4	S	Fwd with LF	
B	7	1	Q	Fwd RF (toe-out 1/4 Trn R)	
	8	2	Q	Fwd LF (curving 1/4 Trn R)	UA
	9	3 & 4	S	Fwd RF (pivot 1/2 Trn R)	
C	10	1	Q	Sd with LF	1HH
	11	2	Q	Close RF to LF (WC)	CL
	12	3 & 4	S	Fwd with LF	

DVD LESSON:

Your DVD rumba chapters includes a segment featuring the Underarm Turn.

FOLLOWING THE UNDERARM TURN LEAD

When your partner releases his Right-Hand Hold and raises your own right hand (on Step 7), he is letting you know that he is about to lead you into a turn under his left hand. The actual turn is executed in just two steps (Steps 8 and 9). Most dancers will execute this turn as two consecutive pivot turns. Others, however, will execute the step as forward spot turn—a circular movement during which feet pass each other.

Rumba Dance Pattern No. 5

The Cross Body Lead

TIMING: 4/4
RHYTHM: QQS
NUMBER OF COUNTS: 16
NUMBER OF ACTUAL STEPS: 12
CHARACTERISTICS: There are several unique characteristics to this pattern: the breaking of CL Dance Position; the ability to be led by using various hand-holds; a pivot turn danced by the woman after she moves across the front of her partner's body.

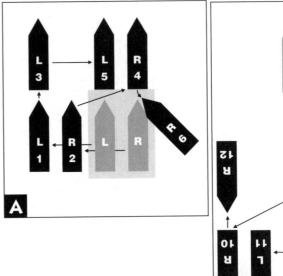

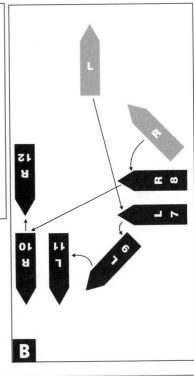

LEADING A CROSS BODY LEAD

There are various ways by which to lead this movement, but all call for you to start turning your body to the left as you step back (Step 6). This toe-in Back Step is the first of two steps that will place you into a LO Position, clearing the path for you to lead your partner to continue walking forward.

As you dance a side step (Step 7), it is important that you continue turning your body to the left because that's what will lead your partner into a teo pivot turn which will then allow you to get back into Closed Dance Position with her.

Box	Step	Count	Rhythm	M—Foot Placement	DP
A	1	1	Q	Sd with LF	CL
	2	2	Q	Close RF to LF (WC)	
	3	3 & 4	S	Fwd with LF	
	4	5	Q	Sd with RF	
	5	6	Q	Close LF to RF (WC)	
	6	7 & 8	S	Bk with RF (toe-in 1/4 Trn L)	
B	7	9	Q	Sd with LF	LO
	8	10	Q	Close RF to LF (WC)	CL
	9	11 & 12	S	Fwd with LF (toe-out 1/2 Trn to L)	
	10	13	Q	Sd with RF	
	11	14	Q	Close LF to RF (WC)	
	12	15 & 16	S	Bk with RF	

Rumba Dance Pattern No. 5

The Cross Body Lead

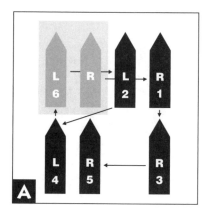

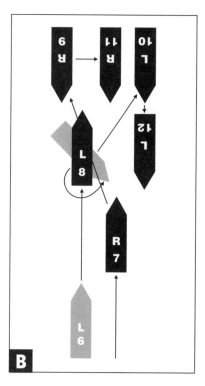

TIMING: 4/4
RHYTHM: QQS
NUMBER OF COUNTS: 16
NUMBER OF ACTUAL STEPS: 12
CHARACTERISTICS: There are several unique characteristics to this pattern: the breaking of CL Dance Position; the ability to be led by using various hand-holds; a pivot turn danced by the woman after she moves across the front of her partner's body.

Box	Step	Count	Rhythm	M—Foot Placement	DP
A	1	1	Q	Sd with RF	CL
	2	2	Q	Close LF to RF (WC)	
	3	3 & 4	S	Bk with RF	
	4	5	Q	Sd with LF	
	5	6	Q	Close RF to LF (WC)	
	6	7 & 8	S	Fwd with LF	CL
B	7	9	Q	Fwd with RF	LO
	8	10	Q	Fwd with LF (pivot 2 to L)	CL
	9	11 & 12	S	Bk with RF	
	10	13	Q	Sd with LF	
	11	14	Q	Close RF to LF (WC)	
	12	15 & 16	S	Fwd with LF	

DVD LESSON:

Your DVD segment breaks down the Cross Body Lead as well as a number of dance holds that can be danced to lead in and out of it.

Chapter 10

The Salsa and the Mambo

For a beginner, there is practically no difference between the basic steps of the mambo and the basic steps of its more contemporary off-shoot, the salsa. In fact, their only difference lies on the beat on which dancers start. Traditionally, ballroom dance instructors have always danced and taught the mambo by taking the first step as a forward step on the 2nd beat of a 4/4 musical measure, the "2" count. On the other hand, salsa dancers take that same first step on the first beat of the measure, the "1" count.

The mambo, a fusion of American swing and Cuban rumba, became the dance rage during the forties when Perez Prado and his orchestra played Mambo No. 5 at the famous Tropicana Nightclub, one of the first night spots American tourists flocked to when visiting Havana. But it was in the late forties at a New York City nightclub, The Palladium, where mambo spread to the rest of the U.S.

Salsa's actual origin breeds a certain amount of debate. But everyone agrees that salsa was popularized by orchestras and singing artists from Puerto Rico, New York and Miami—all three cities with large Hispanic communities. Among these orchestras one of the most influential in the development of salsa songs and rhythms is the orchestra of the late

Tito Puente who many saw in the movie *The Mambo Kings*. But few Latin singing artists have been as identified with salsa music and lyrics as the legendary Celia Cruz who left Cuba in the 1960s and became the most internationally acclaimed Latin singer of our times, earning the title of "The Queen of Salsa."

Today, there are a number of popular dance instructors, especially in New York City, who have spent a lot of years and effort reviving the mambo in its original "on 2" count. But at cities all across the United States it is salsa danced on the "1" or "3" count that younger generations know and dance. It is mainly for that reason that salsa is what I feature in this chapter, regardless of the fact that during my ballroom competition days the mambo was not only one of my favorite dances, it was also the first dance my parents taught me.

That having been said, there is now a chance that you could be asking yourself, "What if someone asks me to dance a mambo?" You answer, "Yes." Then, you listen to the music, letting a couple of bars go by, and you start any of the dance patterns you've learned here taking your first step on the "2" beat. It is that simple!

Fundamental Elements of the Salsa

FOOTWORK

Salsa footwork follows the general rule of all footwork in Latin dances: ball/flat on forward and back step and inside edge of the foot to whole foot on all side steps.

weight is distributed over to the ball of the foot as you press, most of the body's weight remains on the other foot (the supporting foot).

Then, as the upper body continues to lean forward onto the pressing foot, the heel lowers, the foot flattens and the knee straightens under the full impact of the body's weight.

Salsa footwork on forward and backward steps.

Salsa footwork on side steps.

Relation Between Footwork and Weight Shifting Action

As in all Latin dances, the shifting of weight from one weight-bearing step (or supporting foot) onto the next weight-bearing step (or moving foot), involves a mechanical chain reaction that starts with the feet and ends with the hips.

First, the ball of the traveling foot is placed on the dance floor, pressing down on it with its corresponding knee at a bent angle. Although some

One quick way to feel and understand the mechanics involved during this weight-shifting action is to climb up a couple of steps of a flight of stairs. As you take the first step, the ball of the foot is placed down first. Its corresponding knee is in a bent position. Your body then leans forward over the thigh of the bent knee to climb the step, exerting downward pressure on the ankle and entire foot. The downward pressure of the body's weight causes the knee to straighten as you finally climb that one step.

Position of feet in a forward step's mid-stride.

As the weight shifts onto the foot, its knee straightens.

When stepping sideways, we shift the weight by first placing or pressing down on the inside edge of the moving foot. Then, again, as the full weight of the body is transferred onto that foot its corresponding knee straightens and, for a moment, the body is standing tall. But as we take the next step, the hip of the straightened leg shifts farther outwards and the entire process starts all over again.

When stepping back, the weight-shifting process is almost identical to that which takes place as we step forward, but in reverse and not with as much hip action.

TIMING AND RHYTHM

The musical measure of the salsa has four beats: 4/4. Most social level salsa dance patterns take two measures (8 counts) to complete. However, only six steps (foot placements) are performed during those 8 counts. Two steps use one count each (a "Quick" rhythm). One step uses two counts (a "Slow" rhythm).

Just to give you a peek into the difference between the salsa and the mambo, here's a comparative breakdown of the foot placements of both the salsa and the mambo during their identical progressive basic step.

Forward and Back Breaks to Salsa and Mambo Timing/Rhythm (T/R)

Step	Salsa T/R	Mambo T/R	M & W—Foot Placement
1	1 / Q	2 / Q	Step Fwd with LF
2	2 / Q	3 / Q	Step Bk In-Pl with RF
3	3 & 4 / S	4 & 1 / S	Close LF to RF (WC)
4	1 / Q	2 / Q	Step Bk with RF
5	2 / Q	3 / Q	Step Fwd In-Pl with LF
6	3 & 4 / S	4 & 1 / S	Close RF to LF (WC)

DANCE STANCE, FRAME, POSITIONS AND HOLDS

Latin dances are all about isolated, rhythmically expressive, movements of the shoulders, rib cage, hips and knees—none of which could be performed were dancers to maintain a smooth dance-like dance stance or frame. Instead, their dance frame has to be more relaxed with elbows kept down and alongside the body. However, Latin dancers must keep a forward-leaning upper body stance which keeps their body weight over the front part of the feet.

Forward-leaning salsa stance.

In salsa, as in all Latin dances, a dancer's body maintains a slight, forward-leaning stand throughout. This allows for better hip and rib cage motion—two characteristics of the Cuban motion. This stand also

allows dancers to maintain more of their body weight over the front part of the feet.

In salsa, dance positions frequently change within a pattern or while linking patterns. The dance positions featured in this chapter's patterns are as follows.

Closed Dance Position (CL)

There is no body contact between partners. Generally, partners stand about a foot apart facing each other.

The woman's left hand is placed either on the side of the man's right arm, just below the shoulder joint. The palm of her right hand is in contact with the palm of the man's left hand with the fingers loosely closed over the base of the man's left index finger.

Salsa dancers.

The man's right hand is held under the woman's left shoulder blade. His fingers should stay close, but men lead with the outer edge of the right hand not with the fingers. (Little bothers a woman as much as feeling her partner's fingers digging into her back.)

The man's left hand is held off to the side at about chest level and with the elbow bent. The man's left hand is a place where his partner rests her hand. It is not what the man uses to grab or hold onto his partner.

Partners in a salsa One-Hand Hold.

Couple's salsa dance frame.

Just as partners may change dance positions within a dance pattern, they often also change dance holds. The dance holds of the patterns featured in this chapter are as follows.

Open Dance Position–One-Hand Hold (1HH)

Partners stand farther apart with the palm of the woman's right hand resting on the palm of the man's left hand. The free hands can be held in a variety of positions, but the most common is off to the side for the woman and off to the side or next to the body with the elbow bent for the man.

Open Dance Position–Two-Hand Hold (2HH)

Partners are holding each other with opposite hands.

DANCE PATTERN BUILDING BLOCKS

The salsa is a "spot dance." It can be danced in a stamp-size space with partners exchanging dance positions and dance holds, swirling moves, and underarms turns.

Salsa dance patterns consist of short sequences of individual steps, none of which are difficult to learn. The difference between the dance's signature dance patterns and its more advanced ones lie not on intricate pattern choreography but on the ability of dancers to lead or to follow multiple turns, spins, and

Partners in a salsa Two-Hand Hold.

changes of hand position holds which are led into from two dance patterns: the progressive basic and the cross body lead. All in all, this is a dance that is open to individual interpretation and expression as it is related to a rainbow of cultural tastes in music and folklore.

While the mambo is often included in professional and amateur ballroom competitions sanctioned by many dance associations that share similar or identical dance pattern curriculums, the salsa is seldom included in those competitions. However, there are several dance associations which hold salsa competitions across the world and have developed a number of dance pattern syllabuses to which competitors adhere to. But, as previously mentioned, even some of those patterns can vary in timing, rhythm, foot placement and in the individual interpretation and styling of dance teams.

The salsa's pattern building blocks are as follows.

Rocking Steps Forward, Back and Side

In dance terminology, rocking steps are called "break steps" or "breaks" because they consist of small, single steps, generally one or two, during which the dancer steps in any of the three directions then, after a quick shift of weight, steps right back to the starting position. It is sort of like driving your car forward a couple of feet, stepping on the brake, and then immediately putting it in reverse and driving back to where you started from.

There is, however, a difference between a "break step" and a "rocking step." The latter generally consist of two or more steps during which the dancer keeps his body balanced between feet that are placed either one in front of the other or side-by-side. He then rocks his weight between both feet. A rocking movement can be danced in one of two ways: by actually raising and placing the feet off and back on the same spot (moving "In-Pl"), or by leaving both feet on the floor but using a forward and back motion of his upper body and hips to shift weight.

A rocking step.

Forward and Back Rock/Breaks:

Step	M & W—Foot Placement
1	Fwd with LF
2	Bk In-Pl with RF
3	Close LF to RF (WC)
4	Bk with RF
5	Fwd In-Pl with LF
6	Close RF to LF (WC)

Side-to-Side Rock/Breaks:

Step	M & W—Foot Placement
1	Sd with LF
2	Sd In-Pl with RF
3	Close LF to RF (WC)
4	Sd with RF
5	Sd In-Pl with LF
6	Close RF to LF (WC)

Dancer shows a left hip moving left as right foot moves right.

Latin "Walks"

There's not a lot of "walking" that takes place in salsa dance patterns. At most, dancers will take one or two forward or backward steps to link rock/breaks (as in the case of a cross body lead). Yet, even these short duration steps must adhere to the characteristic ball/flat footwork and to the correct hip-shifting motion—the Cuban motion.

Pivots, Swivels, and Spins

A pivot is a turn that's executed on the ball of a weight-supporting foot. Most pivots are done in 1/4 to 1/2 degree turns to the left or to the right. In Latin dance terminology we often use the term "a Chase turn" to describe what is in fact a pivot turn.

A swivel, however, can be either a turn of the feet and body, generally a 1/8 turn, or just a turn the feet make in preparation for a spin. In a spin, a dancer pivots 1/2 to a full turn on a weight-supporting foot.

Cross Overs

A Cross Over is a forward break danced with both partners facing the same direction. Generally, a Cross Over is preceded by a side step, with partners facing each other in Closed Dance Position, then pivoting either to the left or to the right (LO or RO) in order to allow one foot to cross over the side step and then dance a cross over break.

Partners in Left Open, 1HH, dance position during a Cross Over Break.

CHARACTERISTIC STYLING OF THE SALSA

Cuban Hip Motion

Because of their origins, the characteristic body motions of the salsa, the rumba and of cha-cha are known as Cuban motion.

I've heard some people say that when it comes to Latin dances "It's all in the hips." In some ways, this is true. The movement of the hips is what accentuates the beats and musical instruments of Latin music (bongos, claves and conga drums).

I've also heard it said that those not born or raised in Latin cultures can never move their hips like Latin folks. I will admit that the authentic hip and body movements come easier to us, but only because we've been brought up listening to Latin music or, as in my own case, brought up watching my parents do an unbelievable mambo. Yet I have worked with people of all nationalities and know from experience that with practice your hips can learn to move with as much authenticity as any native Latin.

The simplest way I have found for beginners to get their feet, knees and hips working together and, ultimately, get their entire body moving with an authentic Latin dance rhythmic look is through the following exercise. Please, try it often. I always made my students start their lessons with it.

1. Start with feet apart and the body's weight equally distributed (50/50) between both feet, keeping both knees slightly bent.

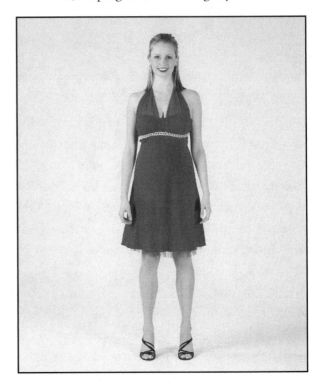

Starting position.

2. Shift the right hip over to the right leg, letting the leg straighten as the hip settles over it.

Hip shifts in opposite direction as weight shifts again.

3. Now, shift the left hip over to the left leg, letting that leg straighten as the hip settles over it.

Hip shifts sideways over weight-supporting leg.

4. Try doing this several times. At every try, see if you can keep your upper body as much in-between both feet as possible. By the way, the only way you are going to accomplish that is by keeping your rib cage from moving over to either side, thus isolating your hips from the rest of the upper body.

Now let's go a couple of steps further.

1. Start with feet apart and the body's weight equally distributed (50/50) between both feet, keeping both knees slightly bent.

2. Shift the right hip over to the right leg again. However, this time, as your right hip settles over the straightened right leg, let the knee of the left leg draw the left foot over to the right foot. It should feel as if the right hip's settling action is what ultimately draws the moving foot toward the supporting foot.

3. Ok. Now, let the left side of your upper body (the rib cage) lean sideways toward the left foot, applying some pressure on that foot. Then, place the entire foot on the floor while you shift your right hip over to it, freeing the right foot of the body's weight.

Knee/hip relation on weight-shifting movement.

Rib cage and knee/hip relation on weight-shifting movement.

Try repeating the above exercise by performing four to six continuous side steps, paying attention to how the feet, the knees and the hips interact during the shift of weight. Before you know it, you will be moving the Latin way.

The 50/50 Rule of Latin Dance Lead and Follow

When a man and a woman are dancing together, it is the man who, of course, leads the pattern. There's such a thing, however, as women who tend to back-lead their partners into patterns. On the other hand, it is the woman who through her body movements and individualized styling makes the dance, especially salsa. Moreover, without an equal share, a 50/50 communication system between partners, one or both will find themselves pushing or pulling the other.

In salsa, there's also an added lead and follow element. It is called "visual lead" or "follow." There's no technical description I can provide for this element, for it relies on how attentive and responsive each partner is to the movements of the other's head and eyes.

For example, during dance patterns where partners stay in Closed Dance Position, and are thus facing each other, it is much easier for either partner to both see and feel, and thus mirror, each other's movement. This makes it much easier for the woman to perceive an oncoming change in lead or direction. On the other hand, during turns or multiple spins where focal points change at rapid speed it is very important that partners keep as much eye contact as possible. Doing so will help a woman gauge her position in relation to her partner's position and the distance or amount of space she can cover while spinning. It also allows the man to shadow his partner's movement closely and therefore to "be there for her" at the moment the spin is finished.

A woman's wrists are possibly her best tool of communication, especially when dancing in Closed Dance Position. Because of their placement—left hand on man's shoulder or on the seam of his jacket's sleeve, and right hand in contact with his left hand—it is through the wrists of her hands that she first gets a sense of any upcoming changes in body movement or direction. Meaning, her wrists must always be on the alert!

Her wrists also play a major role when her partner decides to change dance positions or dance position holds, such as suddenly changing from a Closed Position to a One- or Two-Hand Hold. Needless to say, regardless of how adept a woman is at sensing a partner's oncoming lead, there's little she can feel or sense if her partner's own body and hand movements are not communicating the proper message. This is why when working with men I often emphasize that regardless of the dance or the dance pattern being performed, *it is always the body as a unit that needs to communicate an upcoming lead, not the hands or the feet. They come second.*

In all Open Positions, the fingers of the woman's right or left hand always face down and are placed over the fingers of the man's right or left hand which always face upwards, connecting into a hinge-like position. This position is often referred to as "palm-to-palm."

In the palm-to-palm hold, the palm of the man's hand faces upwards. The palm of the woman's hand faces downward.

If Walls Could Talk

Here's a simple exercise that will help you feel and understand how the body, the wrists, elbows and forearms interact to communicate and sense a dance lead.

1. Face a wall and step back away from it at arm's-length.
2. Place the fingertips of both hands on the wall at about waist level.
3. Bend your knees, slightly.
4. Lean forward from the waist, letting your elbows and wrist feel some of the body's forward-leaning pressure.
5. Keeping your elbows pointing down and at equal distance from each other, bend your right knee directly over the front of your right foot. At the same time, let your right shoulder and right side of your rib cage move closer to the wall. You should feel your weight shifting more over to your right side. You should also feel more pressure being exerted on your wrists and fingers as you move closer to the wall.

That's the sort of communication I'm talking about. If the wall could talk, it would tell you that it feels the right side of your body coming closer to it and the left side of the body backing away.

If you were doing this exercise with a friend or dance partner—and you should—you should do it with your eyes shut close. You would then sense each other's movement and shift of weight, as long as both of you kept that even, light forward pressure on your wrists and elbows.

When you are in a One- or Two-Hand Hold, feeling that 50/50 degree of communication is a lot easier. It is when you're leading or following a turn, especially an underarm that it is tougher to maintain that bilateral firmness.

In such cases, it is the woman's fingers that keep the lead-and-follow communication going by staying extended, but close, and pressing against the palm of the man's open hand.

In underarm turns, the man's open left hand acts as a wall of support for his partner. It's almost as if, once she senses the lead, she pushes herself away from the hand into the turn only to find the hand again for support when she completes the turn.

Position of hands during an underarm turn.

Salsa Two-Hand Hold.

Salsa Dance Pattern No. 1

Forward and Back Breaks

TIMING: 4/4
RHYTHM: QQS
NUMBER OF COUNTS: 8
NUMBER OF ACTUAL STEPS: 6
CHARACTERISTICS: Weight Changes (WC) whenever the traveling foot closes (comes together) to the supporting foot.

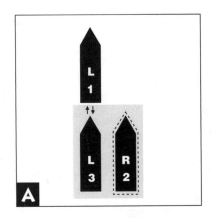

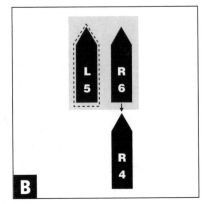

DANCE TIP:

Your salsa DVD tutorial starts with an explanation of the breaks. While the combined breaks form a dance pattern, it is not one that you would find yourself doing with any frequency once you are more familiar with the dance and its rhythms. However, it is the best pattern for practicing Cuban motion and for getting used to the 4-count Latin beat and rhythm.

BOX	STEP	COUNT	RHYTHM*	M—FOOT PLACEMENT
A	1	1	Q	Fwd with LF
	2	2	Q	Bk In-Pl with RF
	3	3 & 4	S	Close LF to RF (WC)
B	4	5	Q	Bk with RF
	5	6	Q	Fwd In-Pl with LF
	6	7 & 8	S	Close RF to LF (WC)

* To make it easier for beginners to dance the single count forward and back breaking steps (Counts 1, 2, 5, 6) followed by their linking, double-count step (Counts 3 & 4, 7 & 8), many teachers also opt to call out salsa patterns in Quick and Slow rhythms.

Salsa Dance Pattern No. 1

Forward and Back Breaks

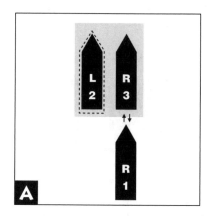

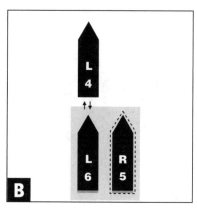

TIMING: 4/4
RHYTHM: QQS
NUMBER OF COUNTS: 8
NUMBER OF ACTUAL STEPS: 6
CHARACTERISTICS: Weight Changes (WC) whenever the traveling foot closes (comes together) to the supporting foot.

Box	Step	Count	Rhythm*	W—Foot Placement
A	1	1	Q	Bk with RF
	2	2	Q	Fwd In-Pl with LF
	3	3 & 4	S	Close RF to LF (WC)
B	4	5	Q	Fwd with LF
	5	6	Q	Bk In-Pl with RF
	6	7 & 8	S	Close LF to RF (WC)

* To make it easier for beginners to dance the single count, forward and back breaking steps (Counts 1, 2, 5, 6) followed by their linking, double-count step (Counts 3 & 4, 7 & 8), many teachers also opt to call out salsa patterns in Quick and Slow rhythms.

M Salsa Dance Pattern No. 2

Side-to-Side Breaks

TIMING: 4/4
RHYTHM: QQS
NUMBER OF COUNTS: 8
NUMBER OF ACTUAL STEPS: 6
CHARACTERISTICS: Weight Changes (WC) whenever the traveling foot closes (comes together) to the supporting foot.

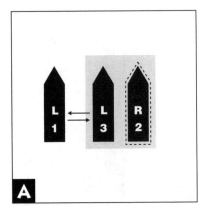

A

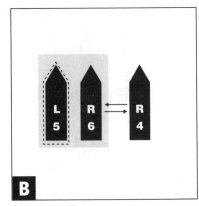

B

DANCE TIP:

Your salsa DVD tutorial starts with an explanation of the breaks. While the combined breaks form a dance pattern, it is not one that you would find yourself doing with any frequency once you are more familiar with the dance and its rhythms. However, it is the best pattern for practicing Cuban motion and for getting used to the 4-count Latin beat and rhythm.

Box	Step	Count	Rhythm*	M—Foot Placement
A	1	1	Q	Sd with LF
	2	2	Q	Sd In-Pl with RF
	3	3 & 4	S	Close LF to RF (WC)
B	4	5	Q	Sd with RF
	5	6	Q	Sd In-Pl with LF
	6	7 & 8	S	Close RF to LF (WC)

* To make it easier for beginners to dance the single count, forward and back breaking steps (Counts 1, 2 ,5, 6) followed by their linking, double-count step (Counts 3 & 4, 7 & 8), many teachers also opt to call out salsa patterns in Quick and Slow rhythms.

Salsa Dance Pattern No. 2

Side-to-Side Breaks

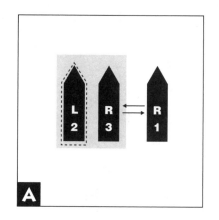

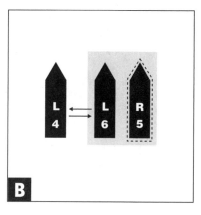

TIMING: 4/4
RHYTHM: QQS
NUMBER OF COUNTS: 8
NUMBER OF ACTUAL STEPS: 6
CHARACTERISTICS: Weight Changes (WC) whenever the traveling foot closes (comes together) to the supporting foot.

Box	Step	Count	Rhythm*	W—Foot Placement
A	1	1	Q	Sd with RF
	2	2	Q	Sd In-Pl with LF
	3	3 & 4	S	Close RF to LF (WC)
B	4	5	Q	Sd with LF
	5	6	Q	Sd In-Pl with RF
	6	7 & 8	S	Close LF to RF (WC)

* To make it easier for beginners to dance the single count, forward and back breaking steps (Counts 1, 2, 5, 6) followed by their linking, double–count step (Counts 3 & 4, 7 & 8), many teachers also opt to call out salsa patterns in Quick and Slow rhythms.

Salsa Dance Pattern No. 3

The Open Break

TIMING: 4/4
RHYTHM: QQS
NUMBER OF COUNTS: 8
NUMBER OF ACTUAL STEPS: 6
CHARACTERISTICS: Weight Changes (WC) whenever the traveling foot closes (comes together) to the supporting foot.

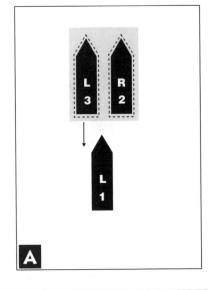

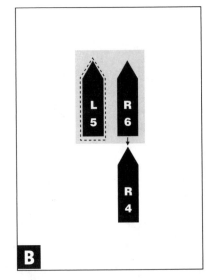

Couple in open break.

Box	Step	Count	Rhythm	M—Foot Placement	DP
A	1	1	Q	Bk with LF	1HH
	2	2	Q	Fwd In-Pl with RF	
	3	3 & 4	S	Close LF to RF (WC)	
B	4	5	Q	Bk with RF	
	5	6	Q	Fwd In-Pl with LF	
	6	7 & 8	S	Close RF to LF (WC)	

DANCE TIP:

Your salsa DVD tutorial starts with an explanation of the breaks. While the combined breaks form a dance pattern, it is not one that you would find yourself doing with any frequency once you are more familiar with the dance and its rhythms. However, it is the best pattern for practicing Cuban motion and for getting used to the 4-count Latin beat and rhythm.

Salsa Dance Pattern No. 3

W

The Open Break

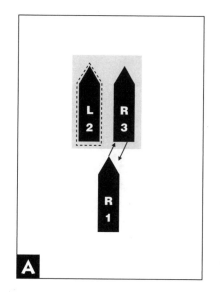

TIMING: 4/4
RHYTHM: QQS
NUMBER OF COUNTS: 8
NUMBER OF ACTUAL STEPS: 6
CHARACTERISTICS: Weight Changes (WC) whenever the traveling foot closes (comes together) to the supporting foot.

Box	Step	Count	Rhythm	W—Foot Placement	DP
A	1	1	Q	Bk with RF	1HH
	2	2	Q	Fwd In-Pl with LF	
	3	3 & 4	S	Close RF to LF (WC)	
B	4	5	Q	Fwd with L	
	5	6	Q	Bk In-Pl with RF	
	6	7 & 8	S	Close LF to RF (WC)	

Salsa Dance Pattern No. 4

The Progressive Basic

Timing: 4/4
Rhythm: QQS
Number of counts: 8
Number of actual steps: 6
Characteristics: Two sets of Breaks linked by a walking step. This is the dance pattern that's most danced within one dance set and the one most danced to lead into other dance patterns.

DANCE TIP:

Generally, men start dancing this pattern in Closed Dance Position, but it can also be danced with One- and Two-Hand Hold or in Apart Position. This dance pattern is also danced with partners making gradual counterclockwise turns.

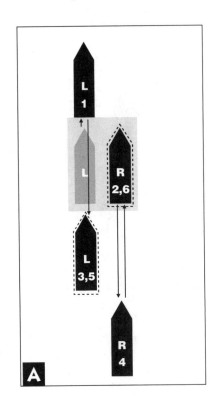

Box	Step	Count	Rhythm	M—Foot Placement
A	1	1	Q	Fwd with LF
	2	2	Q	Bk In-Pl with RF
	3	3 & 4	S	Bk with LF
	4	5	Q	Bk with RF
	5	6	Q	Fwd In-Pl with LF
	6	7 & 8	S	Fwd with RF

Salsa Dance Pattern No. 4

The Progressive Basic

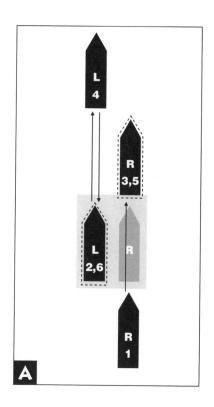

TIMING: 4/4
RHYTHM: QQS
NUMBER OF COUNTS: 8
NUMBER OF ACTUAL STEPS: 6
CHARACTERISTICS: Two sets of Breaks linked by a walking step. This is the dance pattern that's most danced within one dance set and the one most danced to lead into other dance patterns.

Box	Step	Count	Rhythm	W—Foot Placement
A	1	1	Q	Bk with RF
	2	2	Q	Fwd In-Pl with LF
	3	3 & 4	S	Fwd with RF
	4	5	Q	Fwd with LF
	5	6	Q	Bk In-Pl with RF
	6	7 & 8	S	Bk with LF

Salsa Dance Pattern No. 5

The Cross Body Lead

TIMING: 4/4
RHYTHM: QQS
NUMBER OF COUNTS: 8
NUMBER OF ACTUAL STEPS: 6
CHARACTERISTICS: In its most basic form, partners start in CL Position, move into LO Position and back into CL.

DANCE TIP:

This pattern can be led from various types of dance positions and dance holds, but mainly from Closed Dance Position and One- or Two-Hand Hold. Regardless, it is both the man's left hand and his stepping back and away from his partner's path that will signal an upcoming cross body lead. Men, remember the 50/50 Rule of Partnering.

The man's left hand lowers to below the level of his waist and turns slightly inward on Step 3 of the pattern.

When dancing in Closed Dance Position, the man can opt to also guide his partner across the line of his body with slight right-hand pressure on her back.

When dancing with a Two-Hand Hold, both hands can then guide her, but it is the man's left hand that does most of the leading.

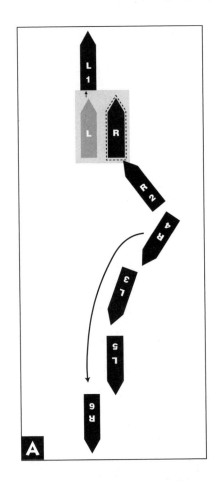

Box	Step	Count	Rhythm	M—Foot Placement	CL
A	1	1	Q	Fwd with LF	CL
	2	2	Q	Bk with RF (toe-in 1/4 to L)	
	3	3 & 4	S	Sd with LF	LO*
				(1/4 turn toe-out to L)	
	4	5	Q	Fwd with RF (toe-in 1/2 to L)	
	5	6	Q	Fwd with LF	CL
	6	7 & 8	S	Fwd with RF	
*Left Open.					

Salsa Dance Pattern No. 5

W

The Cross Body Lead

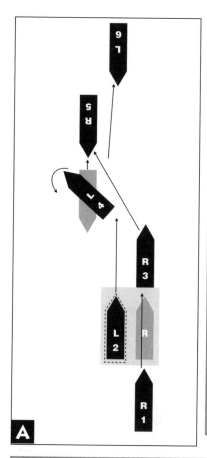

TIMING: 4/4
RHYTHM: QQS
NUMBER OF COUNTS: 8
NUMBER OF ACTUAL STEPS: 6
CHARACTERISTICS: In its most basic form, partners start in CL Position, move into LO Position and back into CL.

Box	Step	Count	Rhythm	W—Foot Placement	CL
A	1	1	Q	Bk with RF	CL
	2	2	Q	Fwd In-Pl with LF	
	3	3 & 4	S	Fwd with RF	LO*
	4	5	Q	Fwd with LF (toe-out pivot 1/2 to L)	
	5	6	Q	Bk with RF	CL
	6	7 & 8	S	Bk with LF	

*Left Open.

DANCE TIP:

Most Latin dances share this dance pattern. In salsa, the Cross Body Lead is especially popular because it is the pattern that leads dancers into the most variety of turns and spins.

For the man, the Cross Body Lead is quite a simple step. He's actually dancing nothing other than a Progressive Basic during which he turns to his left on Step 2 (Count 2), stepping away from his partner's line of dance.

For the woman, the Cross Body Lead is the pattern that first allows her a myriad of individual arm and body styling moves. It is also the first pattern of this series where she learns to pivot to the left on her left foot on Step 4 (Count 5).

From start to finish, the Cross Body Lead is danced in 6 foot placements with partners ending up having exchanged places at the sixth step.

The Cross Body Lead can be danced with partners in a Closed Position dance hold as well as in a One- or Two-Hand Hold.

Salsa Dance Pattern No. 6

The Underarm Turn

TIMING: 4/4

RHYTHM: QQS

NUMBER OF COUNTS: 8

NUMBER OF ACTUAL STEPS: 6

CHARACTERISTICS: This dance pattern uses the Progressive Basic as a lead-in movement. In order to set up the lead for the Underarm Turn the man must change dance position holds from CL to 1HH on Step 4 of the Progressive Basic. Once the woman has completed the UA Turn, couple can return to CL Dance Position as they wrap up the movement with another Progressive Basic.

DANCE TIP:

You can prepare this pattern by first leading into it with a full Progressive Basic or as shown by going straight into it.

The performance of smooth turns largely depends on the man's expertise with quick changes of hand holds and dance positions. But it is also the woman's own dance proficiency with the techniques of turning and spinning that count a lot. In addition, she must be constantly conscious not only of where her partner is at while she's turning, but also of keeping her turning movements tight and compact—always within the framework of the space provided to her by her partner.

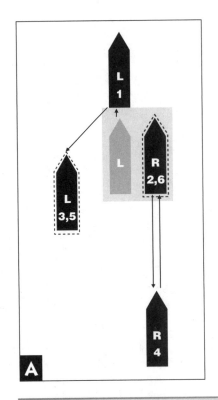

Box	Step	Count	Rhythm	M—Foot Placement	DP
A	1	1	Q	Fwd with LF	1HH
	2	2	Q	Bk In-Pl with RF	
	3	3 & 4	S	Sd with LF	
B	4	5	Q	Bk with RF	UA
	5	6	Q	Fwd In-Pl with LF	
	6	7 & 8	S	Fwd with RF	1HH

Salsa Dance Pattern No. 6

W

The Underarm Turn

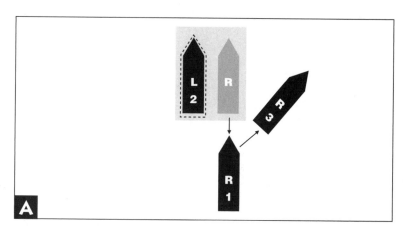

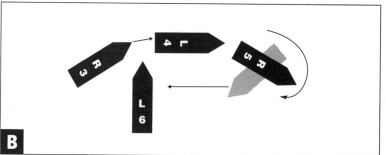

TIMING: 4/4
RHYTHM: QQS
NUMBER OF COUNTS: 8
NUMBER OF ACTUAL STEPS: 6
CHARACTERISTICS: This dance pattern uses the Progressive Basic as a lead-in movement. In order to set up the lead for the Underarm Turn the man must change dance position holds from CL to 1HH on Step 4 of the Progressive Basic. Once the woman has completed the UA Turn, couple can return to CL Dance Position as they wrap up the movement with another Progressive Basic.

DVD LESSON:

Turn to your DVD tutorial for more about the patterns listed above and for practicing them to salsa music.

Box	Step	Count	Rhythm	W—Foot Placement	DP
A	1	1	Q	Bk with RF	1HH
	2	2	Q	Fwd In–Pl with LF	
	3	3 & 4	S	Fwd with RF (toe-out 1/4 to R)	
B	4	5	Q	Fwd with LF (pivot 3/4 to R)	UA
	5	6	Q	Fwd with RF (pivot 1/8 to R)	
	6	7 & 8	S	Sd with LF	1HH

Chapter 11

The Cha-cha

When it became popular in the mid-fifties, this Cuban dance was called the cha-cha-cha because it was danced to a slower-tempo mambo pattern to which a triple-step (syncopated) sequence had been added between each forward and backward set of mambo breaks.

Every one knows that the cha-cha is as Cuban as Ricky Ricardo. But there's a good possibility that while the cha-cha's roots are unquestionably Afro-Cuban, the choreographic structure of the American version of its patterns and dance positions might have been somewhat influenced by the lindy/swing which was popular in the U.S. in the late forties and early fifties. Certainly, the cha-cha's signature syncopated triple step and the swing's syncopated triple step are kissing cousins.

As far as social-level dance patterns go, the difference between cha-cha and mambo steps is found only in the sequence of triple steps that link each rock/break step. The perfect cha-cha tempo is a slower tempo mambo: 30 to 32 MPM. Ballroom style cha-cha dancers prefer a faster tempo than do native Latin dancers, none of whom dance the triple step by moving the feet forward and back. Instead, they mark the triple rhythm with weight changes in place.

Fundamental Elements of the Cha-cha

FOOTWORK

Like the salsa and the rumba, the cha-cha's basic footwork is described as Ball/Flat, keeping the body's weight over the front part of the foot. In all steps, the feet, ankles, knees, hip and upper body work in total synchronicity to provide the characteristic Cuban hip motion. However, it is much tougher to keep the hips moving as much during the pattern's three-step syncopated portion as it is during the rock/break steps. When moving from step to step, the ball of the traveling foot is always kept sliding, or sweeping, on the surface of the dance floor.

TIMING AND RHYTHM

Cha-cha dance music is written in 4/4 timing: 4 beats or counts to every measure of music. Most dance patterns take 8 to 16 counts to complete. The rhythm of the cha-cha dance pattern is a syncopated rhythm. Meaning the fourth beat is split in two in order to accommodate the triple step. Hence the rhythmic count of its dance patterns is 1, 2, 3, 4, &.

While at Latin clubs and parties the cha-cha is nowhere as popular as the salsa, you'll find some dancers mixing cha-cha moves and rhythms with their salsa moves.

Universally, ballroom dance rules call for the cha-cha to be danced on the "2" count. Meaning, every forward and back break is danced on the "2" and the "6" count of an 8 count group.

However, for beginners, this is not an easy rhythm to start dancing on or to maintain while dancing. To them, it is much easier to step on the "1" count, the heaviest and thus most audibly distinguished count. It is for that reason that I have chosen to start our cha-cha patterns with a side step. Often called a "preparation step" this side movement allows beginners to start on the "1" count, but to end up dancing their break steps on the "2" and "6" count, respectively.

Practicing the Cha-Cha Triple Rhythm

Although not a dance pattern you would commonly do on the dance floor, the following pattern is the perfect one for practicing the quick shift of weight that takes place during the syncopated triple step.

Step	Count	M & W—Foot Placement
1	1	Fwd with LF
2	2	Bk In-Pl with RF
3	3	Close LF to RF (WC)
4	&	Step In-Pl with RF (WC)
5	4	Step In-Pl with LF (WC)
6	5	Bk with RF
7	6	Fwd In-Pl with LF
8	7	Close RF to LF
9	&	Step In-Pl with LF (WC)
10	8	Step In-Pl with RF (WC)
Repeat several times.		

While doing this exercise, keep your forward and back break steps short. Do not let your feet come off the floor, especially during the triple step, brushing the balls of the feet on the dance floor at all times. To make this easier for you I'm asking you to break forward and back on the "1" and the "5," a no-no in formal Latin ballroom technique.

Dance Stance, Frame, Positions, and Holds

In the cha-cha, as in all Latin dances, a dancer's body maintains a slight, forward-leaning stand throughout. This allows for better hip and rib cage motion—the two characteristics of the authentic Cuban motion. This stand also allows dancers to maintain more of their body weight over the front part of the feet.

In the cha-cha, dance positions frequently change within a pattern or while linking patterns.

Closed Dance Position (CL)

In the cha-cha's Closed Dance Position partners generally stand farther apart from each other than in the other Latin dances, especially while dancing the cha-cha's forward and back triple step.

The woman's left hand is placed either on the side of the man's right arm, just below the shoulder joint. The palm of her right hand is in contact with the palm of the man's left hand with the fingers loosely closed over the base of the man's left index finger.

The man's right hand is held under the woman's left shoulder blade. His fingers should stay close, but men lead with the outer edge of the right hand not with the fingers. (Little bothers a woman as much as feeling her partner's fingers digging into her back.)

Dance frame of cha-cha.

The man's left hand is held off to the side at about chest level and with the elbow bent. The man's left hand is a place where his partner rests her hand. It is not what the man uses to grab or hold onto his partner.

Dance positions, and I can't emphasize this enough, are not only the manner in which partners stand while dancing. They are also the manner in which partners give each other a space to dance within.

Partners dancing cha-cha triple basic in CL with 2HH.

Open Dance Position—One-Hand Cross Hold (1HH)

Partners stand farther apart with the palm of the woman's right hand resting on the palm of the man's right hand. The free hands can be held in a variety of positions, but the most common is off to the side for the woman and off to the side or next to the body with the elbow bent for the man.

Open Dance Position—Two-Hand Hold (2HH)

Partners are holding each other with opposite hands.

Partners in Open Position with 2HH.

Partners in Open Position with 1HH.

Apart Dance Position

Partners are either facing each other with no hand contact or they are performing a solo spin.

Partners dancing cha-cha basic in Apart Position.

PATTERN BUILDING BLOCKS

The dance pattern building blocks of the cha-cha are:

Rocking Steps Forward and Back

In dance terminology, rocking steps are called "break steps" or "breaks" because they consist of small, single steps, generally one or two, during which the dancer steps in any of the three directions then, after a quick shift of weight, steps right back to the starting position. It is sort of like driving your car forward a couple of feet, stepping on the brake, and then immediately putting it in reverse and driving back to where you started from.

There is however a difference between a "break step" and a "rocking step." The latter generally consists of two or more individual steps during which the dancer keeps his body balanced between feet that are placed either one in front of the other or side by side. He then rocks his weight between both feet. A rocking movement can be danced in one of two ways: by actually raising and placing the feet off and back on the same spot (moving "In-Pl"), or by leaving both feet on the floor but using a forward and back motion of his upper body and hips to shift weight.

Dancer "breaking" forward.   *Dancer moving back to original position.*

Forward and Back Rock/Breaks:

Step	M & W—Foot Placement
1	Fwd with LF
2	Bk In-Pl with RF
3	Close LF to RF (WC)
4	Bk with RF
5	Fwd In-Pl with LF
6	Close RF to LF (WC)

Triple Chassé

A Chassé consists of three consecutive steps that can be danced moving forward, back or sideways at a syncopated rhythm: three steps within 2 counts of music.

STEP	COUNT	M & W—FOOT PLACEMENT
1	1	Sd with LF
2	&	Close RF to LF (WC)
3	2	Sd with LF (reverse direction)
4	3	Sd with RF
5	&	Close LF to RF (WC)
6	4	Sd with RF

Converting Salsa Steps to Cha-Cha Steps

Every pattern that was featured in the salsa chapter can be easily danced as a cha-cha dance pattern by just adding the triple-step sequence between each of the salsa forward and back rock breaks.

CHARACTERISTIC STYLING OF THE CHA-CHA

The triple step is the one element that characterizes the cha-cha and that also distinguishes it from the mambo and the salsa. It is also the element that makes the cha-cha more of a traveling dance, for the triple step can be danced as a short-shuffling movement or as a sequence of longer steps with feet passing each other when moving forward and back.

In the cha-cha, the Cuban hip motion is more accented during rock/breaks than it is during the triple step.

Cuban Hip Motion

Coordinating the placement of the feet and the movement of the knees and hips, while shifting weight from one foot to the other, takes practice. Here's a simple exercise that will help you get them all working together.

1. Start with feet apart and the body's weight equally distributed (50/50) between both feet, keeping both knees slightly bent.

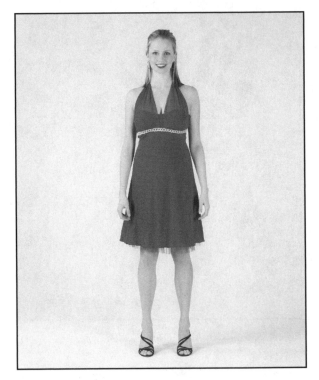

Starting position.

2. Shift the right hip over to the right leg, letting the leg straighten as the hip settles over it.
3. Now, shift the left hip over to the left leg, letting that leg straighten as the hip settles over it.

DVD LESSON:

For a one-on-one tutorial on Cuban motion, please view the Cuban motion segment found in the DVD's Latin Dances section.

Hip shifts in opposite direction as weight shifts again.

Hip shifts sideways over weight-supporting leg.

Now let's go a couple of steps further.

1. Start with feet apart and the body's weight equally distributed (50/50) between both feet, keeping both knees slightly bent.

2. Shift the right hip over to the right leg again. However, this time, as your right hip settles over the straightened right leg, let the knee of the left leg draw the left foot over to the right foot. It should feel as if the right hip's settling action is what ultimately draws the moving foot toward the supporting foot.

3. Ok. Now, let the left side of your upper body (the rib cage) lean sideways toward the left foot, applying some pressure on that foot. Then, place the entire foot on the floor while you shift your right hip over to it, freeing the right foot of the body's weight.

Repeat this exercise several times until you can feel the synchronization between the feet, the knee and the hips as the shift of weight takes place.

Now, let's go a step further. Let's add a rhythmic count to this exercise. Starting with your weight back on your right leg I want you to make five consecutive shifts of weight.

4. Try doing this several times. At every try, see if you can keep your upper body as much in-between both feet as possible. By the way, the only way you are going to accomplish that is by keeping your rib cage from moving over to either side, thus isolating your hips from the rest of the upper body.

Stand with your feet placed slightly apart. Place all of your body's weight on a straight right leg. Keep the knee of your left leg bent and only the ball of the left foot in contact with the floor without placing weight on it.

Move your right hip as far to the right side as it is comfortable at the same time that you press down on the ball of your left foot. (Pressing the left foot down on the floor does not mean shifting the entire weight of the body onto it.) The left knee will remain bent. Your upper body should be leaning forward.

Now, do shift your weight onto the entire left foot by straightening the left knee and bringing the left hip completely over the left leg, but not all the way to the left side. As the left leg straightens under the weight of the body, the heel of the right foot lifts and the right knee bends.

The first two shifts are done to counts "1" and "2." Shifts 3 through 5 (cha-cha-cha) need to be done a bit faster, at a syncopated 1 & 2 rhythm. Once you complete the fifth shift, your right foot will be free to start another shifting set. You're going to find out that it will take you a little time to make the continuous shifts of weight follow the correct rhythm. But persevere. You'll get it.

1. Out loud, count "1" on your first weight shift.
2. Out loud, count "2" on your second weight shift.
3. Out loud, say "cha" on your third weight shift.
4. Out loud, say "cha" again on your fourth weight shift.
5. Out loud, say "cha" one more time on your fifth weight shift.

The 50/50 Rule of Latin Dance Lead and Follow

When a man and a woman are dancing together, it is the man who, of course, leads the pattern. There's such a thing, however, as women who tend to back-lead their partners into patterns. On the other hand, it is the woman who through her body movements and individualized styling makes the dance, especially in salsa. Moreover, without an equal share, a 50/50 communication system between partners, one or both will find themselves pushing or pulling the other. That may be acceptable in mud wrestling, but not in partner dancing.

In the cha-cha, there's also an added lead and follow element. It is called "visual lead" or "follow." There's no technical description I can provide for this element, for it relies on how attentive and responsive each partner is to the movements of the other's head and eyes.

For example, during dance patterns where partners stay in CL Dance Position, and are thus facing each other, it is much easier for either partner to both see and feel, and thus mirror, each other's movement. This makes it much easier for the woman to perceive an oncoming change in lead or direction. On the other hand, during turns or multiple spins where focal points change at rapid speed it is very important that partners keep as much eye contact as possible. Doing so will help a woman gage her position in relation to her partner's position and the distance or amount of space she can cover while spinning. It also allows the man to shadow his partner's movement closely and therefore to "be there for her" at the moment the spin is finished.

A woman's wrists are possibly her best tool of communication, especially when dancing in Closed Dance Position. Because of their placement—left hand on man's shoulder or on the seam of his jacket's sleeve, and right hand in contact with his left hand—it is through the wrists of her hands that she first gets a sense of any upcoming changes in body movement or direction. Meaning, her wrists must always be on the alert!

Her wrists also play a major role when her partner decides to change dance positions or dance position holds, such as suddenly changing from a Closed Position to a One- or Two-Hand Hold. Needless to say, regardless of how adept a woman is at sensing a partner's oncoming lead, there's little she can feel or sense if her partner's own body and hand movements are not communicating the proper message. This is why when working with men I often emphasize that regardless of the dance or the dance pattern being performed, *it is always the body as a unit that needs to communicate an upcoming lead, not the hands or the feet. They come second.*

In all Open Positions the fingers of the woman's right or left hand always face down and are placed over the fingers of the man's right or left hand which always face upwards, connecting into a hinge-like position. This position is often referred to as "palm-to-palm."

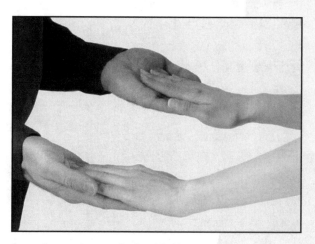

Latin dance palm-to-palm hand hold.

Cha-Cha Dance Pattern No. 1

The Side Basic

TIMING: 4/4
RHYTHM: 1 2 3 4 &
NUMBER OF COUNTS: 8
NUMBER OF ACTUAL STEPS: 10
CHARACTERISTICS: A syncopated triple step wedged betweens two rocking steps is what differentiates the cha-cha from its predecessor, the mambo.

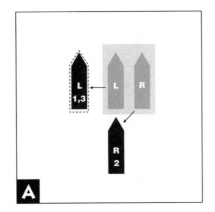

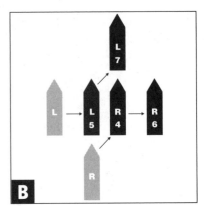

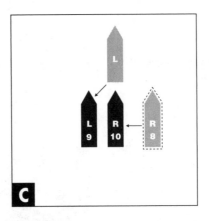

DANCE TIP:

Keep all steps short. Please note that the feet come together during the split fourth count (4 &), making the shift of weight from the moving foot to the supporting foot a quick one. This can be troublesome for beginners as the tendency is to dance this as a skip rather than a smooth but quick shuffle.

Cuban hip motion is the same for the cha-cha as it is for all Latin dances. However, in a faster tempo cha-cha (32 to 34 MPM) hip motion is kept to a minimum during the triple step, but still accented on the rocking/break steps.

Box	Step	Count	M—Foot Placement	DP
A	1	1	Sd with LF	CL
	2	2	Bk with RF	
	3	3	Fwd In-Pl with LF	
B	4	4 (cha)	Sd with RF	
	5	& (cha)	Close LF to RF (WC)	
	6	1 (cha)	Sd with RF	
	7	2	Fwd with LF	
C	8	3	Bk In-Pl with RF	
	9	4 (cha)	Sd with LF	
	10	& (cha)	Close RF to LF (WC)	

Cha-Cha Dance Pattern No. 1

W

The Side Basic

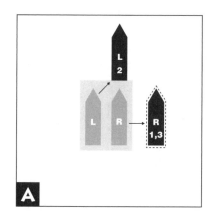

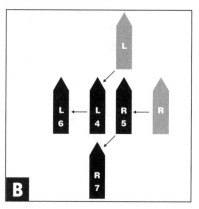

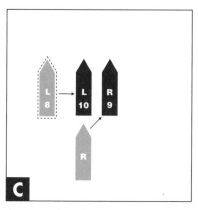

TIMING: 4/4
RHYTHM: 1 2 3 4 &
NUMBER OF COUNTS: 8
NUMBER OF ACTUAL STEPS: 10
CHARACTERISTICS: A syncopated triple step wedged betweens two rocking steps is what differentiates the cha-cha from its predecessor, the mambo.

DANCE TIP:

The first three steps of the cha-cha Side Basic are referred to as the Preparation Step. Most cha-cha patterns start with the Preparation Step and end when the feet come together on the split fourth beat (4 &).

Box	Step	Count	W—Foot Placement	DP
A	1	1	Sd with RF	CL
	2	2	Fwd with LF	
	3	3	Bk In-Pl with RF	
B	4	4 (cha)	Sd with LF	
	5	& (cha)	Close RF to LF (WC)	
	6	1 (cha)	Sd with LF	
	7	2	Bk with RF	
C	8	3	Fwd In-Pl with LF	
	9	4 (cha)	Sd with RF	
	10	& (cha)	Close LF to RF (WC)	

Cha-Cha Dance Pattern No. 2

The Progressive Basic

TIMING: 4/4
RHYTHM: 1 2 3 4 &
NUMBER OF COUNTS: 8
NUMBER OF ACTUAL STEPS: 10
CHARACTERISTICS: A forward and back triple step to a syncopated count wedged between two sets of rocking/break steps.

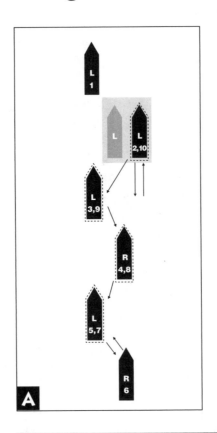

DANCE TIP:

If you've familiarized yourself with the dance's beat and are able to start dancing on the 2 count, you can skip the cha-cha Preparation Step and start to dance the pattern right on the 2 beat as shown here. Just hold the "1" beat and start your break on the "2."

Cha-cha dancers change dance positions all the time. If you are starting your dance with the Side Basic, you will start in Closed Dance Position but can then break into either a One-Hand Hold or Two-Hand Hold Dance Position. You can also choose not to hold your partner and dance it in Apart Dance Position.

Box	Step	Count	M—Foot Placement	DP
		1	Hold the Count	
1	1	2	Fwd with LF	CL
	2	3	Bk in-Pl with RF	
	3	4 (cha)	Bk with LF	
	4	& (cha)	Bk with RF	
	5	1 (cha)	Bk with LF	
	6	2	Bk with RF	
	7	3	Fwd In-Pl with LF	
	8	4 (cha)	Fwd with RF	
	9	& (cha)	Fwd with LF	
	10	1 (cha)	Fwd with RF	

Cha-Cha Dance Pattern No. 2

The Progressive Basic

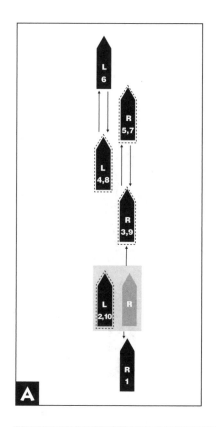

A

TIMING: 4/4
RHYTHM: 1 2 3 4 &
NUMBER OF COUNTS: 8
NUMBER OF ACTUAL STEPS: 10
CHARACTERISTICS: A forward and back triple step to a syncopated count wedged between two sets of rocking/break steps.

DANCE TIP:

If you've familiarized yourself with the dance's beat and are able to start dancing on the 2 count, you can skip the cha-cha Preparation Step and start to dance the pattern right on the 2 beat as shown here. Just hold the "1" beat and start your break on the "2."

Cha-cha dancers change dance positions all the time. If you are starting your dance with the Side Basic, you will start in Closed Dance Position but can then break into either a One-Hand Hold or Two-Hand Hold Dance Position. You can also choose not to hold your partner and dance it in Apart Dance Position.

Box	Step	Count	W—Foot Placement	DP
		1	Hold the Count	
1	2	BK with RF		CL
2	3	Fwd in-Pl with LF		
3	4 (cha)	Fwd with RF		
4	& (cha)	Fwd with LF		
5	1 (cha)	Fwd with RF		
6	2	Fwd with LF		
7	3	BK In-Pl with RF		
8	4 (cha)	BK with LF		
9	& (cha)	BK with RF		
10	1 (cha)	BK with LF		

Cha-Cha Dance Pattern No. 3

The Open Break

TIMING: 4/4

RHYTHM: 1 2 3 4 &

NUMBER OF COUNTS: 8

NUMBER OF ACTUAL STEPS: 10

CHARACTERISTICS: This dance pattern is nothing other than the cha-cha Side Basic started in CL Dance Position and changing to a 1HH just before each partner dances a back rock/breaking step.

DANCE TIP:

Men, an open break has to be preset by you. First, as you dance your first set of triple steps (Steps 4 &5), I recommend that instead of dancing those steps in a straight line you gradually dance them in a diagonal line away from your partner. This allows for a gradual increase of distance between you and your partner. Second, on the second step of that set of triple steps (Step 5-Count "&"), start releasing your right hand from your partner's back and go into a One-Hand Hold. By doing that you won't be too far apart from your partner in your open break.

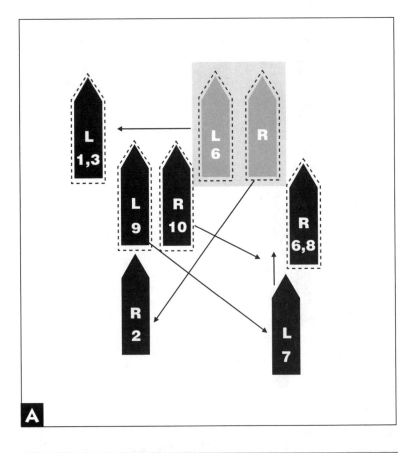

Box	Step	Count	M—Foot Placement	DP
A	1	1	Sd with LF	CL
	2	2	Bk with RF	
	3	3	Fwd In-Pl with LF	
	4	4 (cha)	Sd with RF	
	5	& (cha)	Close LF to RF (WC)	
	6	1 (cha)	Sd with RF	1HH
	7	2	Bk with LF (Open Break)	
	8	3	Fwd In-Pl with RF	
	9	4	Sd with LF	CL
	10	&	Close RF to LF (WC)	

Cha-Cha Dance Pattern No. 3

W

The Open Break

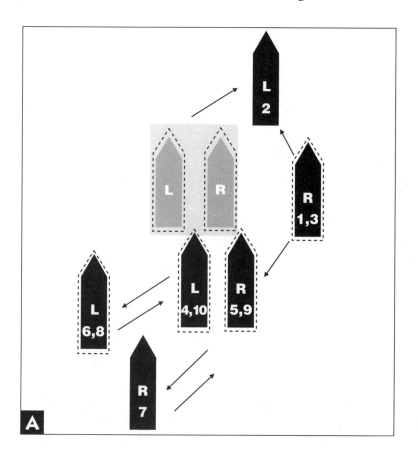

TIMING: 4/4
RHYTHM: 1 2 3 4 &
NUMBER OF COUNTS: 8
NUMBER OF ACTUAL STEPS: 10
CHARACTERISTICS: This dance pattern is nothing other than the cha-cha Side Basic started in CL Dance Position and changing to a 1HH just before each partner dances a back rock/breaking step.

This pattern is the standard lead-in into a variety of other patterns, especially underarm turns. Dance partners stay in Closed Position through the first three steps (the Preparation Step).

Box	Step	Count	W—Foot Placement	DP
A	1	1	Sd with RF	CL
	2	2	Fwd with LF	
	3	3	Bk In-Pl with RF	
	4	4 (cha)	Sd with LF	
	5	& (cha)	Close RF to LF (WC)	
	6	1 (cha)	Sd with LF	1HH
	7	2	Bk with RF	
	8	3	Fwd In-Pl with LF	
	9	4	Step Sd with RF	CL
	10	&	Close LF to RF (WC)	

Cha-Cha Dance Pattern No. 4

The Underarm Turn

TIMING: 4/4
RHYTHM: 1 2 3 4 &
NUMBER OF COUNTS: 12
NUMBER OF ACTUAL STEPS: 20
CHARACTERISTICS: In this pattern the man leads his partner to turn under his left arm. She executes this turn by dancing two pivot movements to the right under his arm and then returning back to a Side Basic, regaining Closed Dance Position.

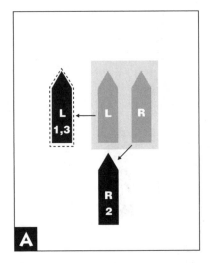

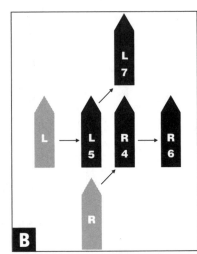

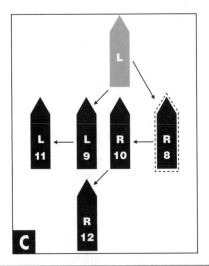

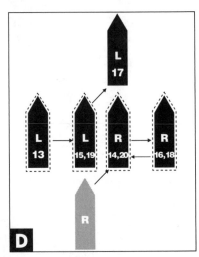

LEADING AND FOLLOWING THE UNDERARM TURN:

This is one of the simplest turns for dance partners to lead and to follow. It calls for the man to let his partner know he's going to lead her into an under arm turn by first releasing his Closed Dance Hold (Step 9) and simultaneously start raising his left hand off to his left side (Step 10) so that he can lead his partner into the underarm pivot turn (Steps 12 and 13). On Step 14, he brings his left hand back down to shoulder-level position, thus ending the turn, and again places his right hand behind his partner back regaining Closed Dance Position.

Cha-Cha Dance Pattern No. 4

The Underarm Turn

Box	Step	Count	M—Foot Placement	DP
A	1	1	Sd with LF	CL
	2	2	Bk with RF	
	3	3	Fwd In-Pl with LF	
B	4	4	Sd with RF	
	5	&	Close LF to RF (WC)	
	6	1	Sd with RF	
	7	2	Fwd with LF	
C	8	3	Bk In-Pl with RF	CL
	9	4	Sd with LF	
	10	&	Close RF to LF (WC)	1HH
	11	1	Sd with LF	
	12	2	Bk with RF	UA
D	13	3	Fwd In-Pl with LF	
	14	4	Sd with RF	CL
	15	&	Close LF to RF (WC)	
	16	1	Sd with RF	
	17	2	Fwd with LF	
	18	3	Bk In-Pl with RF	
	19	4	Sd with LF	
	20	&	Close RF to LF (WC)	

DANCE TIP:

This pattern can be lead from a Side Basic as well as from an Open Break.

Cha-Cha Dance Pattern No. 4

The Underarm Turn

TIMING: 4/4
RHYTHM: 1 2 3 4 &
NUMBER OF COUNTS: 12
NUMBER OF ACTUAL STEPS: 20
CHARACTERISTICS: In this pattern the man leads his partner to turn under his left arm. She executes this turn by dancing two pivot movements to the right under his arm and then returning back to a Side Basic, regaining CL Dance Position.

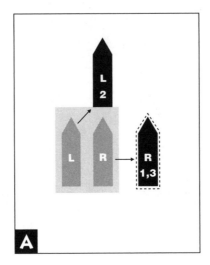

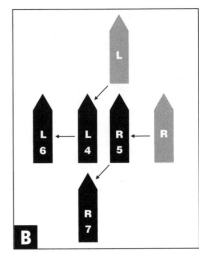

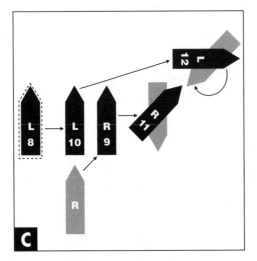

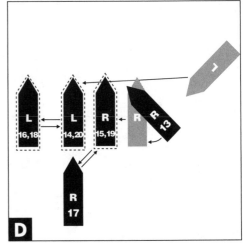

LEADING AND FOLLOWING THE UNDERARM TURN:

This is one of the simplest turns for dance partners to lead and to follow. It calls for the man to let his partner know he's going to lead her into an under arm turn by first releasing his Closed Dance Hold (Step 9) and simultaneously start raising his left hand off to his left side (Step 10) so that he can lead his partner into the underarm pivot turn (Steps 12 and 13). On Step 14, he brings his left hand back down to shoulder-level position, thus ending the turn, and again places his right hand behind his partner back regaining Closed Dance Position.

Cha-Cha Dance Pattern No. 4

W

The Underarm Turn

Box	Step	Count	W—Foot Placement	DP
A	1	1	Sd with RF	CL
	2	2	Fwd with LF	
	3	3	Bk In–Pl with RF	
B	4	4	Sd with LF	
	5	&	Close RF to LF (WC)	
	6	1	Sd with LF	
	7	2	Bk with RF	
C	8	3	Fwd In–Pl with LF	
	9	4	Sd with RF	
	10	&	Close LF to RF (WC)	1HH
	11	1	Sd with RF	
	12	2	Fwd with LF (pivot 3/4 to R)	UA
D	13	3	Fwd with RF (pivot 1/4 to R)	
	14	4	Sd with LF	CL
	15	&	Close RF to LF (WC)	
	16	1	Sd with LF	
	17	2	Bk with RF	
	18	3	Bk In–Pl with LF	
	19	4	Sd with RF	
	20	&	Close LF to RF (WC)	

DANCE TIP:

This pattern can be lead from a Side Basic as well as from an Open Break.

M Cha-Cha Dance Pattern No. 5

The Cross Overs

TIMING: 4/4
RHYTHM: 1 2 3 4 &
NUMBER OF COUNTS: 16
NUMBER OF ACTUAL STEPS: 20
CHARACTERISTICS: This dance pattern combines Cross Over Breaks with different hand position holds and solo pivot turns.

DVD LESSON:

Your cha-cha DVD chapter includes a one-on-one segment featuring all the cha-cha steps featured in this chapter.

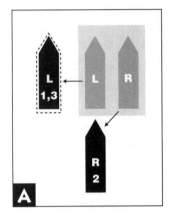

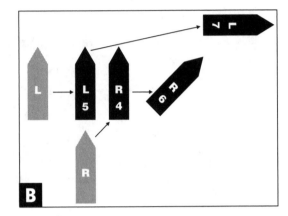

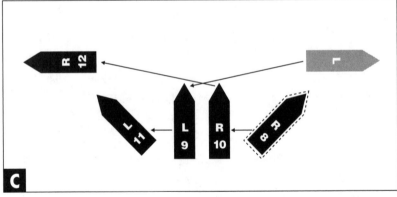

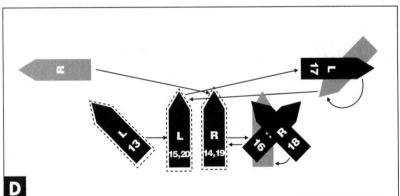

Cha-Cha Dance Pattern No. 5

M

The Cross Overs

Box	Step	Count	M—Foot Placement	DP
A	1	1	Sd with LF	CL
	2	2	Bk with RF	
	3	3	Fwd In-Pl with LF	
B	4	4	Sd with RF	
	5	&	Close LF to RF (WC)	1HH
	6	1	Sd with RF (toe-out 1/3 R)	
	7	2	Fwd with LF (Xover Break)	
C	8	3	Bk In-Pl with RF (toe-in 1/3 L)	
	9	4	Sd with LF	2HH
	10	&	Close RF to LF (WC)	
	11	1	Sd with LF (toe-out 1/3 L)	1HH
	12	2	Fwd with RF (Xover Break)	
D	13	3	Bk In-Pl with LF (toe-in 1/3 R)	
	14	4	Sd with RF	
	15	&	Close LF to RF (WC)	
	16	1	Sd with RF (toe-out 1/3 R)	
	17	2	Fwd with LF (pivot 1/2 to R)	A*
	18	3	Fwd with RF (pivot 1/3 to R)	
	19	4	Sd with LF	CL
	20	&	Close RF to LF (WC)	

*Apart.

DANCE TIP:

For the man, this is a challenging pattern to lead. He must release his right hand from Closed Dance Position (Step 4) and continue to lead his partner into the first Cross Over (Step 7) with just his left hand. After that first Cross Over Break is danced, the man must again use his left hand to lead his partner out of the Cross Over and into the triple step that will lead into the second Cross Over, switching to a Two-Hand Hold for just a couple of counts (Steps 9 & 10) and then taking his partner's left hand into his right hand with a One-Hand Hold to lead her into and out of the second Cross Over (Steps 11–13). He then must change hand holds again (Step 14), this time taking his partner's right hand into his left hand to lead her back in the direction of the first Cross Over. To lead her into the Apart solo turn, all that the man needs to do is to let go of his partner's right hand (Step 17). After both partners complete the pivot turns and get back to facing each other, the man then regains Closed Dance Position.

W Cha-Cha Dance Pattern No. 5

The Cross Overs

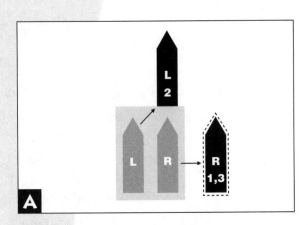

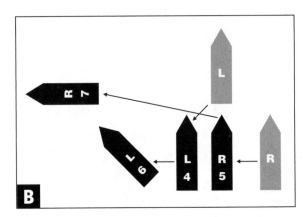

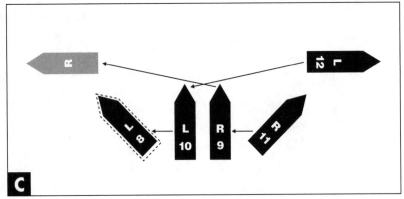

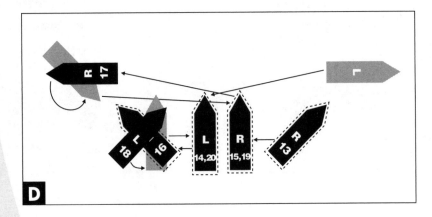

Cha-Cha Dance Pattern No. 5

The Cross Overs

Box	Step	Count	W—Foot Placement	DP
A	1	1	Sd with RF	CL
	2	2	Fwd with LF	
	3	3	Bk In–Pl with RF	
B	4	4	Sd with LF	
	5	&	Close RF to LF (WC)	1HH
	6	1	Sd with LF (toe-out 1/3 L)	
	7	2	Fwd with RF (Xover Break)	
C	8	3	Bk In–Pl with LF (toe-in 1/3 R)	
	9	4	Sd with RF	2HH
	10	&	Close LF to RF (WC)	
	11	1	Sd with RF (toe-out 1/3 R)	1HH
	12	2	Fwd with LF (Xover Break)	
D	13	3	Bk In–Pl with RF (toe-in 1/3 L)	
	14	4	Sd with LF	
	15	&	Close RF to LF (WC)	
	16	1	Sd with LF (toe-out 1/3 L)	
	17	2	Fwd with RF (pivot 2 to L)	A*
	18	3	Fwd with LF (pivot 3 to L)	
	19	4	Sd with RF	CL
	20	&	Close RF to LF (WC)	

*Apart.

Timing: 4/4
Rhythm: 1 2 3 4 &
Number of counts: 16
Number of actual steps: 20
Characteristics: This dance pattern combines Cross Over Breaks with different hand position holds and solo pivot turns.

Chapter 12

The Merengue

The merengue comes from what is now the Dominican Republic, the island Columbus baptized as Hispaniola and that the Dominican Republic shares with Haiti. There's a possibility that it is one of the oldest Latin dances, for some historians date its roots back to when African slaves danced a similar dance which they created by mimicking how their French masters danced the minuet. Another story, and one I heard in Cuba many times, is that it was created during a welcoming party given to a war hero whose wounded leg caused him to limp when he danced. The party's guests, not wanting to humiliate him, started limping as well.

The merengue is a fun dance consisting of long sequences of short side and forward steps. I describe the dance as a vivacious march with Latin hip motion accenting each downbeat with pronounced side motion.

Fundamental Elements of the Merengue

FOOTWORK

The merengue's characteristic footwork is ball/flat. First, you place the ball of the foot on the floor and then you shift the body's weight onto the flat foot.

Because in the merengue hip motion is constant, so is the flexing and straightening action of the ankles and the knees.

Partners dancing merengue.

TIMING AND RHYTHM

Merengue dance music is composed in 8/4 timing: eight counts to each measure of music. Most dance patterns are 16 to 24 counts long with partners stepping in each single musical count.

DANCE POSITIONS

The simplicity of the merengue patterns lends itself to a variety of dance positions and dance position holds. The most common are:

1. Closed Dance Position: In the merengue, Closed Dance Position means closer body contact with partners often dancing in a very tight embrace.

2. Two-Hand Hold: This dance hold is very common in patterns where partners gradually move away from each other, without interrupting their single-count steps, then retrace their steps to get back into Closed Dance Position.

3. Wrap/Cuddle Hold: This dance hold starts from a Two-Hand Hold. The man then leads his partner into an underarm turn maintaining his Two-Hand Hold. The woman ends up wrapped by her partners arms and cuddled off to his right side and in the inside curve of his right elbow.

Partners in merengue 2HH.

Partners in merengue cuddle dance position.

DANCE TIP:

Your merengue DVD chapter includes a segment featuring the Wrap and Cuddle.

PATTERN BUILDING BLOCKS

Merengue dance patterns are all made up of the same foot placements: a constant walk. Although there are no set choreographic standards for the merengue, most all dance patterns consist of long sequences of side-to-side steps, forward or backward steps and spot turns.

CHARACTERISTIC STYLING

What distinguishes the merengue from other dances in the Latin category is the steady rhythmic pulse of its music and its march-like short steps with accented hip action. Unlike most Latin dances, the merengue doesn't feature many rock/breaks in its dance patterns nor do couples frequently break away from their dance holds.

Merengue Dance Pattern No. 1

The Eight Count Basic

TIMING: 8/4

NUMBER OF COUNTS: 8

NUMBER OF ACTUAL STEPS: 8

CHARACTERISTICS: A sequence of eight side-to-side steps with weight changes every time the moving foot closes up to the supporting foot.

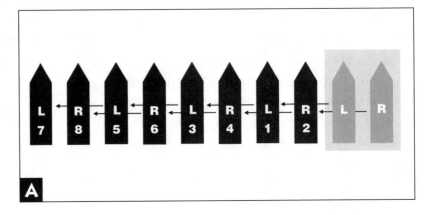

Box	Step	Count	M—Foot Placement
A	1	1	Sd with LF
	2	2	Close RF to LF (WC)
	3	3	Sd with LF
	4	4	Close RF to LF (WC)
	5	5	Sd with LF
	6	6	Close RF to LF (WC)
	7	7	Sd with LF
	8	8	Close RF to LF (WC)

Merengue Dance Pattern No. 1

W

The Eight Count Basic

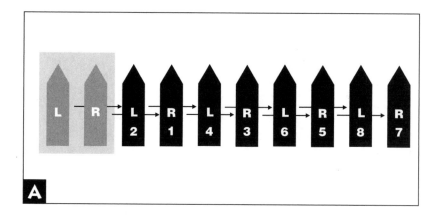

TIMING: 8/4
NUMBER OF COUNTS: 8
NUMBER OF ACTUAL STEPS: 8
CHARACTERISTICS: A sequence of eight side-to-side steps with weight changes every time the moving foot closes up to the supporting foot.

Box	Step	Count	W—Foot Placement
A	1	1	Sd with RF
	2	2	Close LF to RF (WC)
	3	3	Sd with RF
	4	4	Close LF to RF (WC)
	5	5	Sd with RF
	6	6	Close LF to RF (WC)
	7	7	Sd with RF
	8	8	Close LF to RF (WC)

Merengue Dance Pattern No. 2

Forward and Back Walks (Passing the Feet)

TIMING: 8/4
NUMBER OF COUNTS: 8
NUMBER OF ACTUAL STEPS: 8
CHARACTERISTICS: The merengue walks are danced moving forward for the man and back for the woman. There are two ways to dance this pattern. One is by passing the feet. The other is by moving forward on the downbeats (1, 3, 5, 7), closing the moving foot next to the supporting foot on the upbeats (2, 4, 6, 8) and changing weight.

In an additional variation of this dance pattern, the man continues marking the merengue beat with his feet moving In-Pl while he leads his partner to continue marking the beat while she steps back away from him. As she moves back, her hands slide down both of the man's arms and partners end up in a Two-Hand Holds. Once they're both at arm's length, he then leads her to continue dancing her merengue walks back to him.

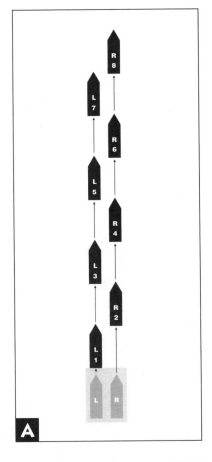

Box	Step	Count	M—Foot Placement	DP
A	1	1	Fwd with LF	CL
	2	2	Fwd with RF	
	3	3	Fwd with LF	
	4	4	Fwd with RF	
	5	5	Fwd with LF	
	6	6	Fwd with RF	
	7	7	Fwd with LF	
	8	8	Fwd with RF	

Repeat Steps 1–8 twice or four times, traveling in a straight line or in a circle.

Merengue Dance Pattern No. 2

W

Forward and Back Walks (Passing the Feet)

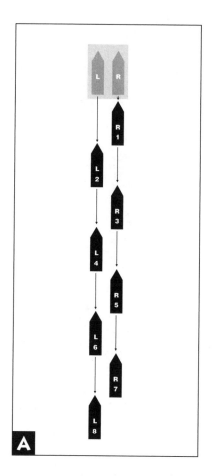

TIMING: 8/4
NUMBER OF COUNTS: 8
NUMBER OF ACTUAL STEPS: 8
CHARACTERISTICS: The merengue walks are danced moving forward for the man and back for the woman. There are two ways to dance this pattern. One is by passing the feet. The other is by moving forward on the downbeats (1, 3, 5, 7), closing the moving foot next to the supporting foot on the upbeats (2, 4, 6, 8) and changing weight.

In an additional variation of this dance pattern, the man continues marking the merengue beat with his feet moving In-Pl while he leads his partner to continue marking the beat while she steps back away from him. As she moves back, her hands slide down both of the man's arms and partners end up in a Two-Hand Holds. Once they're both at arm's length, he then leads her to continue dancing her merengue walks back to him.

Box	Step	Count	W–Foot Placement	DP
A	1	1	Bk with RF	CL
	2	2	Bk with LF	
	3	3	Bk with RF	
	4	4	Bk with LF	
	5	5	Bk with RF	
	6	6	Bk with LF	
	7	7	Bk with RF	
	8	8	Bk with LF	

Repeat Steps 1–8 twice or four times, traveling in a straight line or in a circle.

Merengue Dance Pattern No. 3

Forward and Back Walks (Closing the Feet)

TIMING: 8/4

NUMBER OF COUNTS: 8

NUMBER OF ACTUAL STEPS: 8

CHARACTERISTICS: The merengue walks are danced moving forward for the man and back for the woman. There are two ways to dance this pattern. One is by passing the feet. The other is by moving forward on the downbeats (1, 3 ,5, 7), closing the moving foot next to the supporting foot on the upbeats (2, 4, 6, 8) and changing weight.

In an additional variation of this dance pattern, the man continues marking the merengue beat with his feet moving In-Pl while he leads his partner to continue marking the beat while she steps back away from him. As she moves back, her hands slide down both of the man's arms and partners end up in a Two-Hand Holds. Once they're both at arm's length, he then leads her to continue dancing her merengue walks back to him.

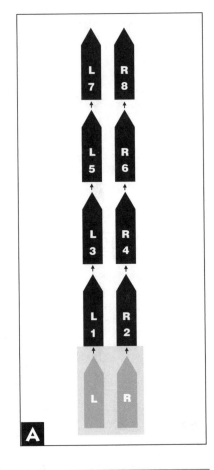

Box	Step	Count	M—Foot Placement	DP
A	1	1	Fwd with LF	CL
	2	2	Close RF to LF (WC)	
	3	3	Fwd with LF	
	4	4	Close RF to LF (WC)	
	5	5	Fwd with LF	
	6	6	Close RF to LF (WC)	
	7	7	Fwd with LF	
	8	8	Close RF to LF (WC)	

Repeat Steps 1–8 twice or four times, traveling in a straight line or in a circle.

Merengue Dance Pattern No. 3 W

Forward and Back Walks (Closing the Feet)

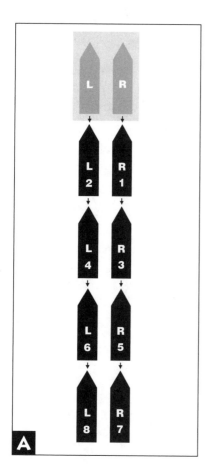

TIMING: 8/4

NUMBER OF COUNTS: 8

NUMBER OF ACTUAL STEPS: 8

CHARACTERISTICS: The merengue walks are danced moving forward for the man and back for the woman. There are two ways to dance this pattern. One is by passing the feet. The other is by moving forward on the downbeats (1, 3, 5, 7), closing the moving foot next to the supporting foot on the upbeats (2, 4, 6, 8) and changing weight.

In an additional variation of this dance pattern, the man continues marking the merengue beat with his feet moving In-Pl while he leads his partner to continue marking the beat while she steps back away from him. As she moves back, her hands slide down both of the man's arms and partners end up in a Two-Hand Holds. Once they're both at arm's length, he then leads her to continue dancing her merengue walks back to him.

Box	Step	Count	W—Foot Placement	DP
A	1	1	Bk with RF	CL
	2	2	Close LF to RF (WC)	
	3	3	Bk with RF	
	4	4	Close LF to RF (WC)	
	5	5	Bk with RF	
	6	6	Close LF to RF (WC)	
	7	7	Bk with RF	
	8	8	Close LF to RF (WC)	

Repeat Steps 1–8 twice or four times, traveling in a straight line or in a circle.

Part Four

The American Rhythm Dances

There are two categories of rhythm dances: the American and the Latin. In both categories, dancers perform a pre-choreographed sequence of dance patterns to musical compositions that are generally structured in sequences of four-musical-beat groups, a 4/4 musical measure. Dancers break body contact, change dance positions and holds, and perform a variety of spins and turns, all while moving their bodies in a myriad of individually expressive ways. The American rhythm dances are the swing and the hustle.

There are three main styles of American swing: East Coast Swing (often referred to as the Triple Swing), the West Coast Swing and the Country Western Swing. All of them evolved from two musical eras, Ragtime and Big Band, which originated dances like the Shag, the Charleston, the Susie "Q" and the Lindy Hop.

The East Coast Swing is the most popular of the three styles. It consists of two continuous sets of triple steps capped by two quick rocking steps and danced to a 6 count rhythm: SSQQ ("1 & 2," "3 & 4," "5," "6").

In the late seventies and early eighties a new American dance craze swept through the U.S. at an amazing speed. The hustle was originally a line dance but was popularized as a partner dance by the movie *Saturday Night Fever*, starring John Travolta. The hustle is all about turns and spins, about exchanging dance positions and dance holds, much like in the West Coast Swing. Today, the hustle is still popular at many dance clubs in Queens and Brooklyn, both boroughs of New York.

Chapter 13

The Swing

At the height of the so-called Roaring Twenties couples "shimmied," "shagged," and "shuffled," all names that were given to the Lindy, also called the Lindy Hop, some say in honor of Charles Lindbergh's first transatlantic flight. The Lindy, considered by many as "too athletic" and even "vulgar," then lost popularity, only to come back in the late thirties boosted by a new musical sound, the swing sound of the Big Band Era.

It was also a time when Latin melodies and dances had gained popularity in the United States, especially the rumba. At the time, the competition between swing and Latin dances was fierce. But the swing allowed for more freedom of individual expression and more innovative choreographic structure and, ultimately, became known as the first original American social dance.

There are three main styles of American swing: East Coast Swing (often referred to as the Triple Swing), the West Coast Swing and the Country Western Swing. The East Coast Swing, characterized by two sets of triple steps capped by two rocking steps, is the most popular of the three styles.

Throughout the states located along our Western seaboard and throughout some of the more inland Southern and Western states, the West Coast Swing is taught at many dance studios. Originally the creation of California dancers, the West Coast Swing takes the most time to learn and to perfect. Often called "push-and-pull" style swing, it consists of a wide array of turning moves during which partners exchange dance positions and dance holds. West Coast swing dance patterns also feature a variety of timing and rhythm changes that can challenge even advance dancers.

Country Western Swing is not as energetic a swing style as its cousins. Dancers not only stay in closed dance position for longer periods of time, but they also move in a counterclockwise direction on the dance floor.

The Jive, the International style version of the American swing, combines many West Coast and East Coast dance patterns. Competition dancers make the Jive quite an exciting and energizing dance to watch, especially when they include in their routines many of the side-by-side dance moves from Big Band era dances.

Although not as popular as it was after World War II, the swing regained some popularity a few years ago when the Gap clothing chain aired a television commercial featuring swing dancers. Swing dancing is not only fun but it has the advantage that its patterns can be danced to most rock, pop and disco melodies.

In this book, I'm featuring only the East Coast Swing because if you wanted to learn just one dance that could get you through 60 percent of the popular songs that are played at parties and nightclubs, the East Cost Swing is it. In addition, most disco music, just like most rock music, is written in 4/4 timing. That is why it is as easy to swing to the Andrews Sisters' "Don't Sit Under the Apple Tree," as it is to swing to Vicky Sue Robinson's "Turn the Beat Around" or Michael Jackson's "Billy Jean."

Fundamental Elements of the East Coast Swing

FOOTWORK

Flexible ankles and knees are the key to good swing dancing. The triple swing consists of two sequences of triple steps followed by a two-step rock/break step. Just about any time that a dance's signature step consists of a syncopated rhythm triple step, the correct footwork is ball/flat on every syncopated triple step and then just the ball of the foot on the breaking step, followed by the whole foot on the subsequent forward rock.

TIMING AND RHYTHM

Swing music is written in 4/4 timing—4 counts to every measure of music. However, the basic dance pattern of the swing uses 6 counts of music not 4. Hence, the completion of the last two steps of the basic pattern, the rocking steps, spills into the first two counts of the succeeding musical measure. Rhythm-wise, swing is broken down into two Slow steps (two counts for each) and two Quick steps (one count for each), making the dance's standard rhythm a SSQQ. However, this standard SSQQ rhythm can also be danced in three different timing sequences: single time, double time and triple time.

The single- and triple-time rhythms are the ones most people dance to. The double-time rhythm is also called Lindy-timing, and is the predominant rhythm of the West Coast-style swing. The tempo of the music is what determines which of the two rhythms dancers should follow. Faster tempos are best danced in single-time. Medium tempos, which is the tempo of most swing melodies, are best danced in triple-rhythm or East Coast Triple Rhythm Swing.

Single-Time Swing

When the tempo of the music being played seems fast, starting your dance with a single-time rhythm basic step is the best way to go. By replacing the syncopated triple step with just two side rocks, you will be dancing in single time. Here's the single-time basic dance pattern.

Timing: 4/4 Number of counts: 6 Number of steps: 4	Step	Count	Rhythm	M—Foot Placement	W—Foot Placement	DP
	1	1 & 2	S	Step Sd L with LF	Step Sd R with RF	CL
	2	3 & 4	S	Step Sd R in-Pl with RF	Step Sd L In-Pl with LF	
	3	5	Q	Rock Bk with LF	Rock Bk with RF	
	4	6	Q	Rock Fwd In-Pl with RF	Rock Fwd In-Pl with LF	

Single Time Swing. Step 1.
M–Step Sd with LF.
W–Step Sd with RF.

Step 2.
M–Step R In-Pl with RF.
W–Step L In-Pl with LF.

Step 3.
M–Rock Bk with LF.
W–Rock Bk with RF.

Step 4.
M–Rock Fwd In-Pl with RF.
W–Rock Fwd In-Pl with LF.

DANCE STANCE, FRAME, POSITIONS, AND HOLDS

The body stance for swing dancing is the most relaxed of all social dance stands. The upper body leans slightly forward to keep most of the body's weight over the front of the feet. In most swing Open Position Dance patterns dancer's hands are held below the waist in a palm-to-palm hand hold.

The Clip Hand Hold.

The steps featured in this chapter call for just three dance positions:

SWING CLOSED DANCE POSITION (CL)

Partners stand facing each other about a foot apart.

Open Dance Position

In many dance patterns, dancers break away from a Closed Position into an Open Position.

Left Open Dance Position

Partners face the same direction. The man's right side of his body and the woman's left side of her body are closer to each other than their respective left and right sides. The feet of both partners point inward toward each other.

One-Hand Hold in palm-to-palm contact during Open Break.

Two-Hand Hold in palm-to-palm contact.

SWING DANCE HOLDS

There are various dance holds. The two featured in our dance patterns are the One-Hand Hold (1HH) and the Two-Hand Hold (2HH). In both, partners' hands are joined by placing the palms of their hands one on top of the other: the palm of the man's hands face up while the palms of the woman's hands face down. This hold is often called "palm-to-palm."

DANCE PATTERN BUILDING BLOCKS

The swing consists of side rocks, forward and back rocks, and side-to-side (triple) walks, all of which are combined and performed according to the tempo of the music being danced to. However, all social-level swing patterns featured in this book can be danced to either single- or triple-time.

CHARACTERISTIC STYLING

Even at a social level, the style of this dance can change according to the individual interpretation of its dancers. Older and more conservative swing dancers and I both tend to swing dance without a lot of hops and jumps. Younger and more adventurous dancers tend to give the swing more of a Lindy Hop look—energetic and athletic. But to learn this dance, the conservative approach is the best. As you progress, you can take all kinds of styling liberties depending, of course, on who you are dancing with. Recently, I attended a wedding where the bride's grandmother asked me to dance the swing with her. I approached our dance with very simple, single-time, basic moves, but not for long. Within a few bars of music this lady was back-leading me into hops, spins and whips, making me break into a sweat as people gathered around us.

Swing is also categorized as a spot dance although not at the level of Latin dances. In its basic signature style, the swing is danced with partners' upper body leaning in the direction of their triple-step sequence, reversing the move at the end of the third step. Rocking steps and breaks are generally danced with an upright posture.

Because partners dance in One-Hand Hold Open Position more often than they do in Closed Dance Position, there are countless styling positions that can be danced by the free arms.

Swing's Magic Linking Steps

The swing's basic patterns A, B, C are this dance's magic steps. They are danced as either the steps that lead into other shorter patterns, like Underarm

Advanced dancers perform swing/hop basic.

Turns, or the steps that link other paterns. The swing Basic A and B can also be danced taking short steps, large steps, hop-like steps (like in the Jive), or turning to both the left and the right.

An Underarm Loop Turn.

M Swing Dance Pattern No. 1

Triple-Step Swing Basic A

TIMING: 4/4
RHYTHM: SSQQ
NUMBER OF COUNTS: 6
NUMBER OF STEPS: 8
CHARACTERISTICS: Side triples are danced with partners' bodies facing each other in CL Dance Position. The first set of triple steps is danced to the left, by the man with his partner dancing it to her right. Directions are then reversed on the second set of triple steps. You can dance this step with three different hand holds.

DANCE TIP:

Keep the distance between steps a short one. Doing so will make the quick transition of direction (Step 4) a lot easier to manage and to perfect. While dancing the two rock/break steps (Steps 5 and 6), keep the feet well under the frame of the body. Too large a distance between rock/break steps will result in a jerky motion. Often, the feet during the rock/breaks will automatically end up in a Fifth Position—front foot pointing toward partner and back foot turned out. This is fine as the foot placement during the rock/breaks is actually dictated by how much of an opening there is between partners' bodies.

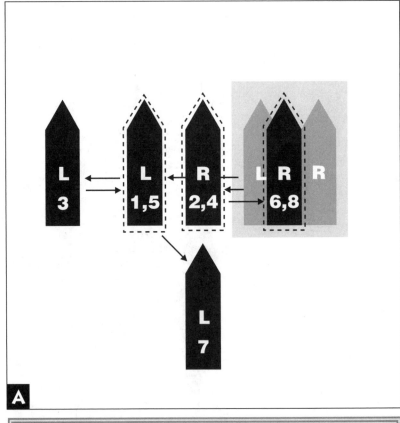

Box	Step	Count	M—Foot Placement	DP
A	1	1	Sd with LF	CL
	2	&	Close RF to LF (WC)	
	3	2	Sd with LF	
			(Reverse direction)	
	4	3	Sd with RF	
	5	&	Close LF to RF (WC)	
	6	4	Sd with RF	
	7	5	Bk with LF	
	8	6	Fwd In-Pl with RF	

Swing Dance Pattern No. 1

W

Triple-Step Swing Basic A

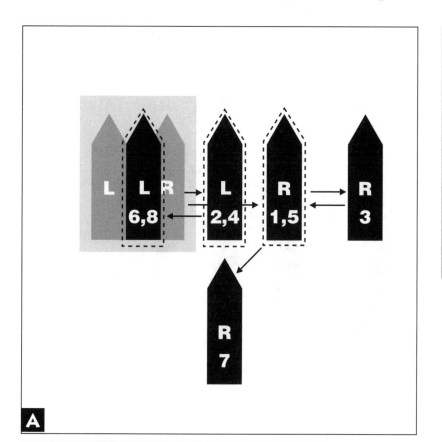

TIMING: 4/4
RHYTHM: SSQQ
NUMBER OF COUNTS: 6
NUMBER OF STEPS: 8
CHARACTERISTICS: Side triples are danced with partners' bodies facing each other in CL Dance Position. The first set of triple steps is danced to the left, by the man with his partner dancing it to her right. Directions are then reversed on the second set of triple steps. You can dance this with three different hand holds.

Box	Step	Count	W—Foot Placement	DP
A	1	1	Sd with RF	CL
	2	&	Close LF to RF (WC)	
	3	2	Sd with RF	
	4	3	Sd with LF (Reverse direction)	
	5	&	Close RF to LF (WC)	
	6	4	Sd with LF	
	7	5	Bk with RF	
	8	6	Fwd In-Pl with LF	

Swing Dance Pattern No. 2

Triple-Step Swing Basic B

TIMING: 4/4
RHYTHM: SSQQ
NUMBER OF COUNTS: 6
NUMBER OF STEPS: 8
CHARACTERISTICS: The only difference between the Triple-Step Swing Basic A and Basic B is that partners start the pattern in LO and remain in LO.

DANCE TIP:

By leading the move with a left-leaning shoulder, the side steps will move diagonally to the left.

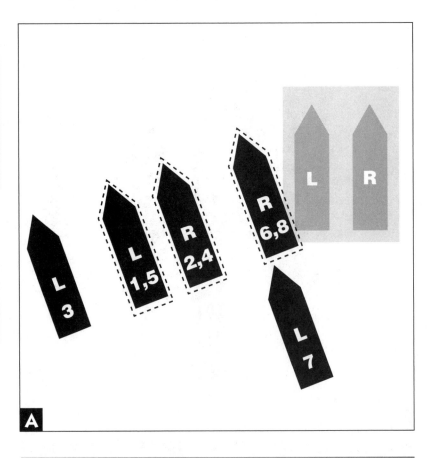

Box	Step	Count	M—Foot Placement	DP
A	1	1	Sd with LF (1/8 Trn L)	LO
	2	&	Close RF to LF (WC)	
	3	2	Sd with LF	
	4	3	Sd with RF	
	5	&	Close LF to RF (WC)	
	6	4	Sd with RF	
	7	5	Bk with LF	
	8	6	Fwd In-Pl with RF	

Swing Dance Pattern No. 2

Triple-Step Swing Basic B

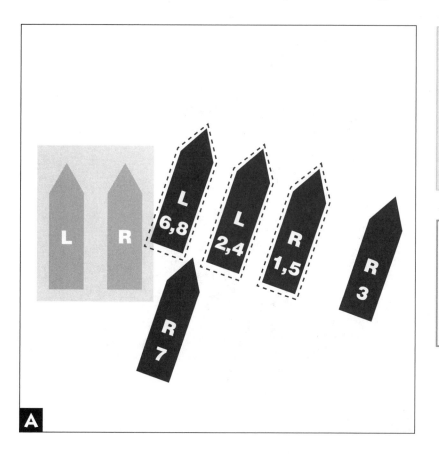

A

TIMING: 4/4
RHYTHM: SSQQ
NUMBER OF COUNTS: 6
NUMBER OF STEPS: 8
CHARACTERISTICS: The only difference between the Triple-Step Swing Basic A and Basic B is that partners start the pattern in LO and remain in LO.

DANCE TIP:

By leaning to the right with the right shoulder, the triple steps will travel diagonally away from your partner.

Box	Step	Count	W—Foot Placement	DP
A	1	1	Sd with RF (1/8 Trn R)	LO
	2	&	Close LF to RF (WC)	
	3	2	Sd with RF	
	4	3	Sd with LF	
	5	&	Close RF to LF (WC)	
	6	4	Sd with LF	
	7	5	Bk with RF	
	8	6	Fwd In–Pl with LF	

Swing Dance Pattern No. 3

Triple-Step Swing Basic C (Left Turning Basic)

TIMING: 4/4

RHYTHM: SSQQ

NUMBER OF COUNTS: 6

NUMBER OF STEPS: 8

CHARACTERISTICS: In this pattern couples make a gradual 1/4 turn to the left. Shoulders lean in the direction of the turn, especially during the first set of triple steps. The difference between this version and the other two is that you will be making a gradual turn to the left during the first set of triple steps. This is the most danced variation of the Triple-Step Swing because it is the variation that leads into most underarm turns and spins. This variation can be danced in either Closed or Left Open Dance Positions.

DANCE TIP:

There are two angles to every turn—an inside and an outside angle.

In this pattern, the man's triple step makes a gradual, 1/8 turn, to the left. He's dancing in the inside angle of the turn—the narrowest angle. Conversely, she's dancing in the outside angle of the turn—the widest angle. If the man doesn't keep the distance between his first set of triple steps a short one, it forces his partner to increase the distance between the first set of her triple steps, making her dancing look rushed.

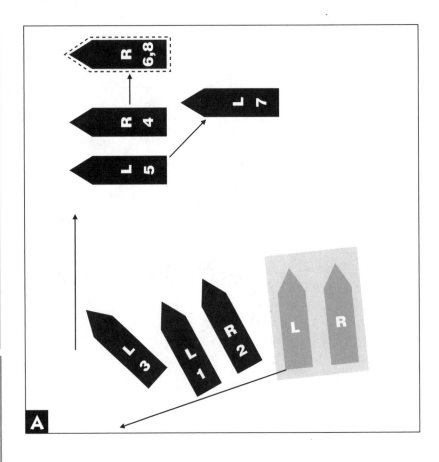

Box	Step	Count	M–Foot Placement	DP
A	1	1	Sd with LF (Trn 1/8 to L)	CL
	2	&	Close RF to LF (WC)	
	3	2	Fwd with LF (Trn 1/8 to L)	
	4	3	Sd with RF	
	5	&	Close LF to RF (WC)	
	6	4	Sd with RF	
	7	5	Bk with LF	
	8	6	Fwd In-Pl with RF	

Swing Dance Pattern No. 3

W

Triple-Step Swing Basic C (Left Turning Basic)

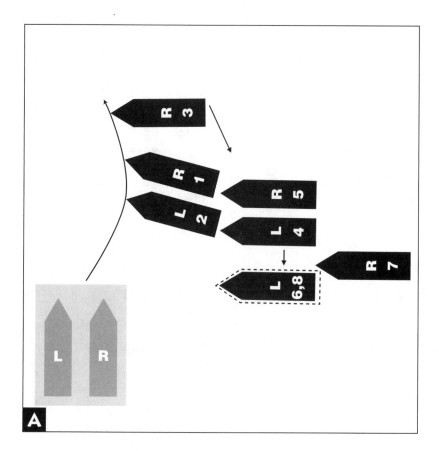

A

TIMING: 4/4
RHYTHM: SSQQ
NUMBER OF COUNTS: 6
NUMBER OF STEPS: 8
CHARACTERISTICS: In this pattern couples make a gradual 1/4 turn to the left. Shoulders lean in the direction of the turn, especially during the first set of triple steps. The difference between this version and the other two is that you will be making a gradual turn to the left during the first set of triple steps. This is the most danced variation of the Triple-Step Swing because it is the variation that leads into most underarm turns and spins. This variation can be danced in either Closed or Left Open Dance Positions.

Box	Step	Count	W—Foot Placement	DP
A	1	1	Sd with RF (toe-in L Trn)	CL
	2	&	Close LF to RF (WC)	
	3	2	Bk with RF (Trn 1/8 to R)	
	4	3	Sd with LF	
	5	&	Close RF to LF (WC)	
	6	4	Sd with LF	
	7	5	Bk with RF	
	8	6	Fwd In-Pl with LF	

M Swing Dance Pattern No. 4

The Open Break

TIMING: 4/4
RHYTHM: SSQQ
NUMBER OF COUNTS: 12
NUMBER OF STEPS: 16
CHARACTERISTICS: On the second step, the side step, the man releases his partner into a One-Hand Hold open dance position. They end up facing each other and dancing a back rock/break step together.

After the open break, partners return to CL Dance Position during the first set of triple sets, making a 1/8 turn to the right on the third of that triple-step sequence. They then finish the dance pattern at the same spot they started in. This is one of swing's signature patterns. It starts with the first two steps of Basic C, turning 1/4 to the left for men, right for women.

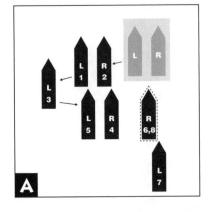

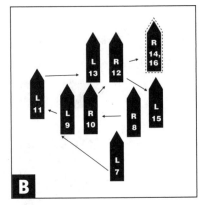

Box	Step	Count	M—Foot Placement	DP
A	1	1	Sd with LF (Clockwise 1/8 Trn to L)	CL
	2	&	Close RF to LF (WC)	
	3	2	Sd with LF (Clockwise 1/8 Trn to R)	
	4	3	Sd with RF	
	5	&	Close LF to RF (WC)	
	6	4	Sd with RF	
	7	5	Bk with LF	1HH
	8	6	Fwd In-Pl with RF	
B	9	1	Sd with LF	CL
	10	&	Close RF to LF (WC)	
	11	2	Sd with LF (Trn 1/4 to R)	
	12	3	Sd with RF	
	13	&	Close LF to RF (WC)	
	14	4	Sd with RF	
	15	5	Bk with LF	
	16	6	Fwd In-Pl with RF	

Swing Dance Pattern No. 4

W

The Open Break

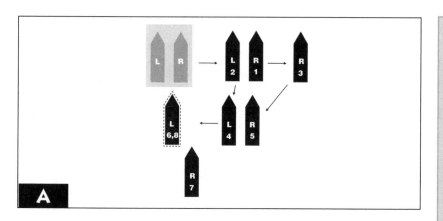

A

TIMING: 4/4
RHYTHM: SSQQ
NUMBER OF COUNTS: 12
NUMBER OF STEPS: 16
CHARACTERISTICS: On the second step, the side step, the man releases his partner into a One-Hand Hold open dance position. They end up facing each other and dancing a back rock/break step together.

After the open break, partners return to CL Dance Position during the first set of triple sets, making a 1/8 turn to the right on the third of that triple-step sequence. They then finish the dance pattern at the same spot they started in. This is one of swing's signature patterns. It starts with the first two steps of Basic C, turning 1/4 to the left for men, right for women.

Box	Step	Count	W—Foot Placement	DP
A	1	1	Sd with RF	CL
			(Counterclockwise 1/8 Trn to R)	
	2	&	Close LF to RF (WC)	
	3	2	Sd with RF	
			(Counterclockwise 1/8 Trn to L)	
	4	3	Sd with LF	
	5	&	Close RF to LF (WC)	
	6	4	Sd with LF	
	7	5	Bk with RF	1HH
	8	6	Fwd In-Pl with LF	
B	9	1	Sd with RF	CL
	10	&	Close LF to RF (WC)	
	11	2	Sd with RF (1/4 Trn to L)	
	12	3	Sd with LF	
	13	&	Close RF to LF (WC)	
	14	4	Sd with LF	
	15	5	Bk with RF	
	16	6	Fwd In-Pl with LF	

DANCE TIP:

Remember: *In partner dancing, the body moves before the feet move.* Especially when a turn is about to be danced, moving the upper body in the direction of the turn is of the utmost importance.

The Open Break is the perfect example of how directions, dance positions, and holds can change quickly within a dance pattern.

Swing Dance Pattern No. 5

The Underarm Turn

TIMING: 4/4

RHYTHM: SSQQ

NUMBER OF COUNTS: 12

NUMBER OF STEPS: 16

CHARACTERISTICS: After dancing a complete Open Break (Steps 1-8), thus ending up in a One-Hand Hold Open Position, the man starts to raise his partner's right arm with his left arm, circling it over his partner's head. As he leads her to circle under his arm, the man continues to dance a Swing Basic A. At the end of this pattern, man can choose to bring his partner back into CL Dance Position or to remain in 1HH Open Position then gradually return to CL Position by dancing another Swing Basic A.

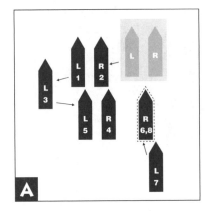

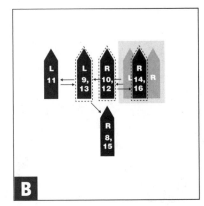

Box	Step	Count	M—Foot Placement	DP
A	1	1	Sd with LF	CL
	2	&	Close RF to LF (WC)	
	3	2	Sd with LF	
	4	3	Sd with RF (Reverse direction)	
	5	&	Close LF to RF (WC)	
	6	4	Sd with RF	
	7	5	Step Bk with LF	1HH
	8	6	Fwd In-Pl with RF	
B	9	1	Sd with LF	
	10	&	Close RF to LF (WC)	UA*
	11	2	Sd with LF	
	12	3	Sd with RF (Reverse direction)	
	13	&	Close LF to RF (WC)	
	14	4	Sd with RF	1HH
	15	5	Bk with LF	
	16	6	Fwd In-Pl with RF	

*Underarm.

Swing Dance Pattern No. 5

The Underarm Turn

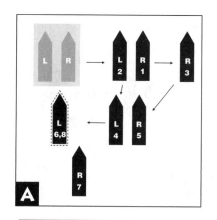

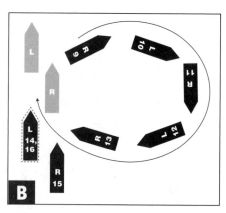

TIMING: 4/4

RHYTHM: SSQQ

NUMBER OF COUNTS: 12

NUMBER OF STEPS: 16

CHARACTERISTICS: In the swing, as well as in most dances, any underarm turn requires that the female partner keep her steps short and maintain her upper body moving in a circular manner until the turn is ended. As most underarm turns are led from a 1HH Open Position, women should also be on the alert whenever their partner starts to raise their hands. Generally, that's an indication that the man intends to lead some type of turn. The first 8 steps of the footprint diagram are those of an Open Break lead-in.

Box	Step	Count	W—Foot Placement	DP
A	1	1	Sd with RF	CL
	2	&	Close LF to RF (WC)	
	3	2	Sd with RF	
	4	3	Sd with LF (Reverse direction)	
	5	&	Close RF to LF (WC)	
	6	4	Sd with LF	
	7	5	Bk with RF	1HH
	8	6	Fwd In–Pl with LF	
B	9	1	Sd with RF (Toe-out 1/8 Trn to R)	
	10	&	Fwd with LF (Start circling UA to R)	UA*
	11	2	Fwd with RF (continue circling UA to R)	
	12	3	Fwd with LF (continue circling UA to R)	
	13	&	Fwd with RF (continue circling UA to R)	
	14	4	Fwd with LF (End of UA turn)	1HH
	15	5	Bk with RF	
	16	6	Fwd In–Pl with LF	

*Underarm.

Swing Dance Pattern No. 6

The Reverse Underarm Turn

TIMING: 4/4
RHYTHM: SSQQ
NUMBER OF COUNTS: 12
NUMBER OF STEPS: 16
CHARACTERISTICS: In this pattern the man dances what is referred to as a spot turn—a tight turn to the left or to the right during which feet make gradual adjustments that can lead to the completion of a full half turn. As the man is performing the spot turn with his feet and body, he is also leading his partner to turn under his left arm to her left. This type of turn ends up placing partners' bodies one behind the other during the first part of the turn (Steps 9–11) with arms forming a sort of "loop." The Open Break is the lead-in pattern of the Reverse Underarm Turn.

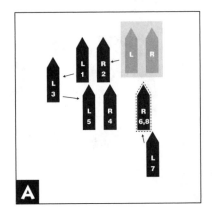

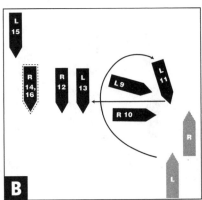

Box	Step	Count	M—Foot Placement	DP
A	1	1	Sd with LF	CL
	2	&	Close RF to LF (WC)	
	3	2	Sd with LF	
	4	3	Sd with RF (reverse direction)	1HH
	5	&	Close LF to RF (WC)	
	6	4	Sd with RF	
	7	5	Bk with LF	
	8	6	Fwd In–Pl with LF	
B	9	1	Sd with LF (start R spot Trn)	UA
	10	&	Close RF to LF (continue gradual R spot Trn)	
	11	2	Sd with LF (continue gradual R spot Trn)	
	12	3	Sd with RF (continue gradual R spot Trn)	
	13	&	Close LF to RF (continue gradual R spot Trn)	
	14	4	Sd with RF (UA Trn is ended)	1HH
	15	5	Bk with LF	
	16	6	Fwd In–Pl with RF	

Swing Dance Pattern No. 6

W

The Reverse Underarm Turn

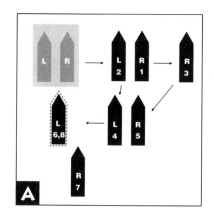

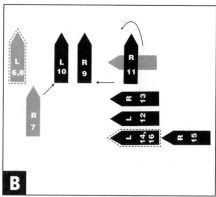

TIMING: 4/4

RHYTHM: SSQQ

NUMBER OF COUNTS: 12

NUMBER OF STEPS: 16

CHARACTERISTICS: The Open Break is the lead-in step for this pattern. Immediately after dancing the last step of the Open Break, the woman is led into a left turning (reverse) Underarm Turn. Characteristically, dancers turn in the direction of their turn's leading foot, i.e., a left turn starts with the left foot, a right turn with the right foot. In this pattern, the exact opposite takes place for the woman. She needs to make a gradual spot turn to the left which starts with her right foot stepping to the side. This movement will end up placing her back directly in front of her partner's body and their respective arms in what is called a "loop" position. From beginning to end this pattern makes a full half turn thus ending up with partners having exchanged their starting dance positions.

Box	Step	Count	W—Foot Placement	DP
A	1	1	Sd with RF	CL
	2	&	Close LF to RF (WC)	
	3	2	Sd with RF	
	4	3	Sd with LF (Reverse direction)	1HH
	5	&	Close RF to LF (WC)	
	6	4	Sd with LF	
	7	5	Bk with RF	
	8	6	Fwd In-PL with LF	
B	9	1	Sd with RF (Toe-in 1/4 Trn to L)	UA
	10	&	Close LF to RF (WC)	UA (loop)
	11	2	Sd with RF (Spin 3/4 Trn to L)	
	12	3	Sd with LF	
	13	&	Close RF to LF (WC)	1HH
	14	4	Sd with LF	
	15	5	Bk with RF	
	16	6	Fwd In-Pl with LF	

Swing Dance Pattern No. 7

The Double Reverse Underarm Turn

TIMING: 4/4

RHYTHM: SSQQ

NUMBER OF COUNTS: 12

NUMBER OF STEPS: 16

CHARACTERISTICS: This is one of the fanciest swing social-level turns. It is best performed once Underarm B is perfected because it calls for the man to also dance a reverse turn under his own arm.

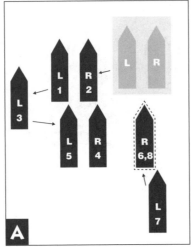

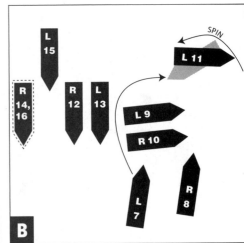

DANCE TIP:

The key to making this step lies on making short steps in a spot-like motion. Immediately following the last step of the Open Break (the lead-in step), the man turns to his right as his left foot steps to the left (Step 9). He then marks the rest of the triple step in a tight spot turn while leading his partner into a Reverse (loop) turn. Once, she has completed her turn, he then spins on his left foot 1/2 turn to his left (Step 11), turning under his own left arm and ending up facing his partner.

Box	Step	Count	M—Foot Placement	DP
A	1	1	Sd with LF	CL
	2	&	Close RF to LF (WC)	
	3	2	Sd with LF	
	4	3	Sd with RF (Reverse direction)	1HH
	5	&	Close LF to RF (WC)	
	6	4	Sd with RF	
	7	5	Bk with LF	
	8	6	Fwd In-Pl with RF	
B	9	1	Sd with LF (Toe-in 1/4 Trn to R)	UA
	10	&	Close RF to LF (WC)	UA (loop)
	11	2	Sd with LF (Spin 3/4 to L)	
	12	3	SD wih RF	
	13	&	Close LF to RF (WC)	1HH
	14	4	Sd with RF	
	15	5	Bk with LF	
	16	6	Fwd In-Pl with RF	

Swing Dance Pattern No. 7

W

The Double Reverse Underarm Turn

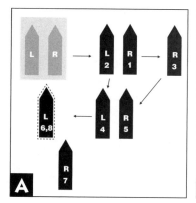

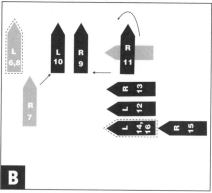

TIMING: 4/4
RHYTHM: SSQQ
NUMBER OF COUNTS: 12
NUMBER OF STEPS: 16
CHARACTERISTICS: For the woman, this pattern is identical to the Underarm B (Reverse Turn) with one exception: the man will turn under his own arm to the left as the woman completes her own reverse turn and goes into her second set of triple steps.

Box	Step	Count	W—Foot Placement	DP
A	1	1	Sd with RF	CL
	2	&	Close LF to RF (WC)	
	3	2	Sd with RF	
	4	3	Sd with LF (Reverse direction)	1HH
	5	&	Close RF to LF (WC)	
	6	4	Sd with LF	
	7	5	Bk with RF	
	8	6	Fwd In-Pl with LF	
B	9	1	Sd with RF (Toe-in 1/4 Trn to L)	UA
	10	&	Close LF to RF (WC)	UA (loop)
	11	2	Sd with RF (Swivel 1/4 Trn to L)	
	12	3	SD wih LF	
	13	&	Close RF to LF (WC)	1HH
	14	4	Sd with LF	
	15	5	Bk with RF	
	16	6	Fwd In-Pl with LF	

DANCE TIP:

From this pattern you can dance the Natural Underarm Turn, the Reverse Underarm Turn and the Double Reverse Underarm Turn.

Chapter 14

The Hustle

Some have said that the Big Band era's swing became the Disco era's hustle. There are some similarities between them, especially when compared with the single-time swing, and when you consider that in both dances partners are constantly exchanging directions, placements and dance positions. But in terms of footwork, timing/rhythm or signature patterns they have nothing in common. In fact, in many ways the hustle is more like the salsa than any other partner dance.

Before becoming a partner dance, the hustle was a line dance which became the craze in 1975 after the release of Van McCoy and the Soul City Symphony's "Hustle." It was not until the 1977 release of the movie *Saturday Night Fever* that the hustle's popularity as a partner dance blossomed. But as a national dance craze its fame started to dwindle quite rapidly.

Today, the hustle's popularity is limited to clubs in two of New York City's boroughs: Brooklyn and Queens. In New York City and other major U.S. cities the hustle is often taught at dance studios under various titles, such as Partner Disco Dancing, Nightclub Disco Dancing, etc.

FOOTWORK

The hustle is a fast dance characterized by compact turning moves. Dance patterns are danced stepping with body's weight shifting from the ball of the foot to the whole foot much like most rhythm dances. Flexible ankles and knees are the key to good dancing.

TIMING AND RHYTHM

Hustle, like most disco tunes, is phrased in 4/4 timing. However, like the swing, the hustle's signature pattern is timed to a six-count format during which 8 individual foot placements are danced. The hustle's foot placement rhythm is a syncopated one: & 1 2 3 & 4 5 6.

DANCE STANCE, FRAME, POSITIONS, AND HOLDS

In the characteristic hustle dance position partners face each other in a Two-Hand Hold, frequently changing into One-Hand Hold and Cross-Hand Hold.

DANCE PATTERN BUILDING BLOCKS

The hustle's signature step is a unique one. It consists of a back rock/break danced at a syncopated rhythm, followed by a forward step and two quick changes of weight (a ball/change move). Good hustle dancers turn, pivot, swivel and spiral around each other without ever staying put in one spot for more than 3 counts of music.

CHARACTERISTICS

Hustle dance patterns can be danced in a small area or they can travel across the room. The speed of the music and its pattern quick shift of weight makes it almost impossible to figure out when a pattern ends and another begins. Leading and following the hustle takes constant awareness of your partner's moves and position, especially during the fast spin turns that good hustle dancers never cease to stop doing. When you watch good hustle dancers, you get the impression that the man is at the intersection of two crisscrossing lanes, a slot, directing his partner to circle around him before she moves to a different slot.

The hustle dance stance.

Hustle Reverse Loop Turn.

Hustle Dance Pattern No. 1

The Basic Time Step

TIMING: 4/4

RHYTHM: & 1 2 3

NUMBER OF COUNTS: 3

NUMBER OF STEPS: 4

CHARACTERISTICS: Tight movements in close body proximity although no body contact. Arms move as fast as the feet do, opening outward and then closing inward with elbows bent within three counts of music.

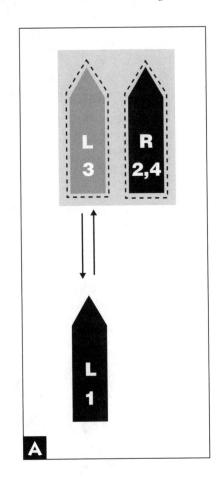

Standard Closed Dance Position.

Box	Step	Count	M—Foot Placement
A	1	&	Rock Bk with LF
	2	1	Rock Fwd In-Pl with RF
	3	2	Close LF to RF (WC)
	4	3	Step In-Pl with RF (WC)

Hustle Dance Pattern No. 1

W

The Basic Time Step

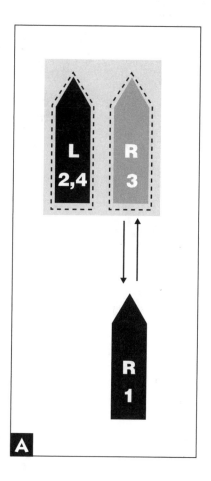

TIMING: 4/4
RHYTHM: & 1 2 3
NUMBER OF COUNTS: 3
NUMBER OF STEPS: 4
CHARACTERISTICS: Tight movements in close body proximity although no body contact. Arms move as fast as the feet do, opening outward and then closing inward with elbows bent within three counts of music.

Box	Step	Count	W—Foot Placement
A	1	&	Rock Bk with RF
	2	1	Rock Fwd In-Pl with LF
	3	2	Close RF to LF (WC)
	4	3	Step In-PL with LF (WC)

Hustle Dance Pattern No. 2

Changing Places

TIMING: 4/4

RHYTHM: & 1 2 3

NUMBER OF COUNTS: 4

NUMBER OF STEPS: 4

CHARACTERISTICS: Most hustle moves travel clockwise. In this signature pattern, partners exchange slots, each rotating 1/2 turn to their right every 3 counts. The tempo of the music and the speed to which the feet must move make it essential that partners maintain their bodies well within the frame of their Two-Hand Hold.

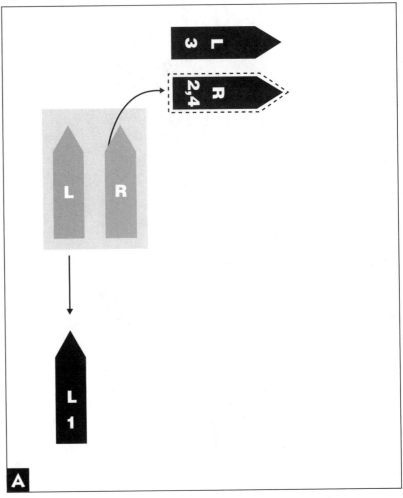

Steps 1 & 2.

Box	Step	Count	M—Foot Placement
A	1	&	Rock Bk with LF
	2	1	Step Fwd (Toe-out 1/2 Trn to R)
	3	2	Step Sd with LF
	4	3	Close RF to LF (WC)

Hustle Dance Pattern No. 2

Changing Places

W

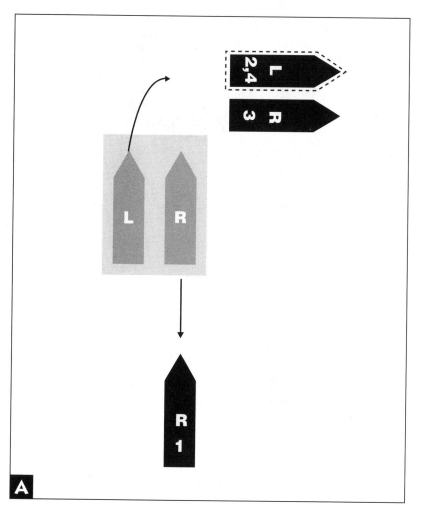

TIMING: 4/4
RHYTHM: & 1 2 3
NUMBER OF COUNTS: 4
NUMBER OF STEPS: 4
CHARACTERISTICS: Most hustle moves travel clockwise. In this signature pattern, partners exchange slots, each rotating 1/2 turn to their right every 3 counts. The tempo of the music and the speed to which the feet must move make it essential that partners maintain their bodies well within the frame of their Two-Hand Hold.

Steps 1 & 2.

Box	Step	Count	W—Foot Placement
A	1	&	Rock Bk with RF
	2	1	Step Fwd with LF (1/2 trn R)
	3	2	Step Sd with RF
	4	3	Close LF to RF (WC)

Hustle Dance Pattern No. 3

Reverse Loop Turn

TIMING: 4/4

RHYTHM: & 1 2 3

NUMBER OF COUNTS: 4

NUMBER OF STEPS: 4

CHARACTERISTICS: This is a simple reverse turn that moves fast with partners exchanging positions during each 3-count set. The speed of it calls for the woman to dance a left pivot turn on Step 1 under her partner's arm. Although the dance pattern consists of only four individual foot placements, dancers generally dance one basic pattern before and after.

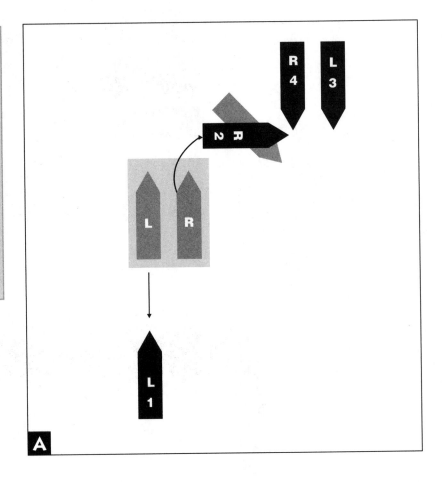

Box	Step	Count	M—Foot Placement
A	1	&	Rock Bk with LF
	2	1	Step Fwd with RF (1/4 trn R)
	3	2	Step Sd with LF (1/4 trn R)
	4	3	Close RF to LF (WC)

Hustle Dance Pattern No. 3

Reverse Loop Turn

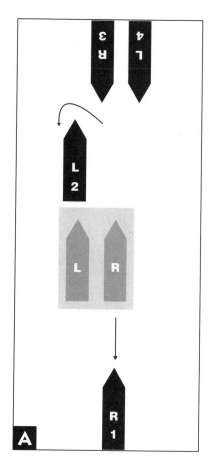

TIMING: 4/4

RHYTHM: & 1 2 3

NUMBER OF COUNTS: 4

NUMBER OF STEPS: 4

CHARACTERISTICS: This is a simple reverse turn that moves fast with partners exchanging positions during each 3-count set. The speed of it calls for the woman to dance a left pivot turn on Step 1 under her partner's arm. Although the dance pattern consists of only four individual foot placements, dancers generally dance one basic pattern before and after.

Arms forming loop in Reverse Loop Turn.

Box	Step	Count	W—Foot Placement
A	1	&	Rock Bk with RF
	2	1	Step Fwd with LF (Spin 1/2 turn L)
	3	2	Step Bk with RF
	4	3	Close LF to RF (WC)

Hustle Dance Pattern No. 4

Hustle Whip

TIMING: 4/4

RHYTHM: & 1 2 3

NUMBER OF COUNTS: 6

NUMBER OF STEPS: 6

CHARACTERISTICS: The whip starts like Pattern #2 (Changing Places), but the man stops his partner before she has a chance to fully rotate 1/2 turn to his right, leading her back to her original spot.

DANCE TIP:

This is the signature pattern that leads women into a variety of turns and solo spins that will have her ending back facing her partner on the same slot she started dancing from.

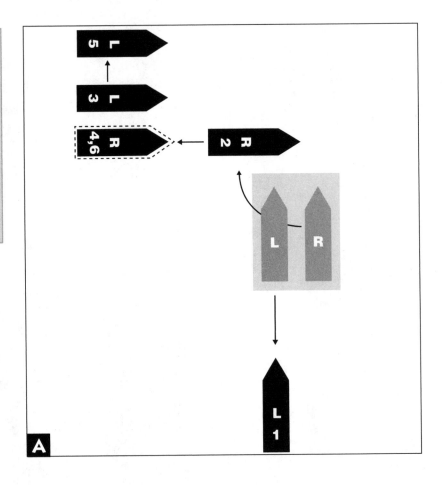

Box	Step	Count	M—Foot Placement
A	1	&	Rock Bk with LF
	2	1	Step Fwd with RF (1/4 trn R)
	3	2	Step Sd with LF
	4	3	Close RF to LF (WC)
	5	&	Rock to the Side with LF
	6	1	Rock to the Side with RF

Hustle Dance Pattern No. 4

Hustle Whip

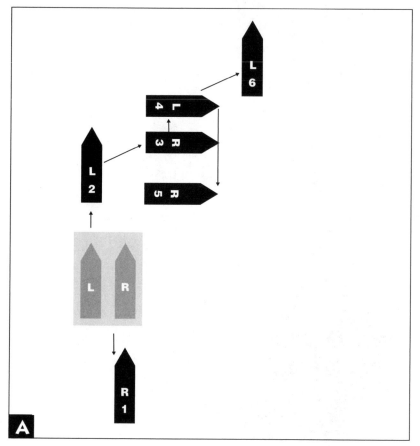

TIMING: 4/4
RHYTHM: & 1 2 3
NUMBER OF COUNTS: 6
NUMBER OF STEPS: 6
CHARACTERISTICS: The whip starts like Pattern #2 (Changing Places), but the man stops his partner before she has a chance to fully rotate 1/2 turn to his right, leading her back to her original spot.

End position of Hustle Whip.

Box	Step	Count	W—Foot Placement
A	1	&	Rock Bk with RF
	2	1	Step Fwd with LF
	3	2	Step Fwd with RF (1/4 trn R)
	4	3	Step Sd with LF (1/4 trn R)
	5	&	Step Sd with RF (whip move)
	6	1	Step Fwd with LF (1/4 trn l)

Part Five

Party and Line Dances

A line dance is a choreographed routine that is performed with men and women standing side-to-side in parallel rows and repeated several times throughout the duration of a song. Many line dances have been created to go with specific songs, although they share a number of the same dance moves, such as grapevines, lock steps, stomps, swivels, etc.

Dancers stand side-by-side on lines and rows with every dancer following the same choreography. Frequently, at the start of the dance, those who best know and perform the specific line dance are found at the front line. Those who might not know the exact choreography stand in the back rows. But as the line dance continues changing lanes and directions, they often find themselves at the front of the line.

The steps and moves within each block of choreography are generally danced to each single count of a song or melody. Some line dances are shorter than others ranging between 24 to 42 total counts and moves. Dancers travel in straight vertical or horizontal lines moving counterclockwise and turning from wall-to-wall, performing different blocks of choreography.

Line dances have been most popular among the country-and-western music crowd, and most line dances have been choreographed to fit specific country songs. But, because line dances are such a fun and easy way to get dancers involved, whether they have a partner or not, some have been created for rock and pop songs as well. The number of line dances is mind-boggling. The line dances you'll be learning in *Let's Dance* come from a group of traditional line dances that are often performed at weddings and parties. But if you ever go to a club known for its line dance parties, one you've never been to before, and hear someone announce the name of one of this book's featured line dances, I suggest that you watch the dancers before you venture into joining them because even the most traditional line dances tend to have variations which can change from one state or region to the next. However, chances are that the version you've learned is not all that different from the one you'll be watching.

Then, the next time the same line dance is played join the group by standing in the middle row. It is the best row because as the line turns you'll always have dancers in front and behind you that you can follow. And one of the greatest things about line dances is that no one will care whether you stomp instead of strike or if you turn instead of vine. As each dancer is on their own, you will be, too.

Chapter 15

Country Line Dances

Most country line dances have been choreographed to fit specific popular country songs. For example, the Tush Push was choreographed by choreographer Melanie Greenwood to "The Achy Breaky Heart," a hit by Billy Ray Cyrus. But you'll find that you can dance the same dance to other songs, as long as they have similar timing and rhythm. In fact, in our DVD, we teach you how to match these line dances to different songs so that you can see how to match the dance to unfamiliar music.

From the 1980s on, as line dances became increasingly popular, the original choreography of many line dances experienced changes and adaptations. Even the title of some line dances change from region to region. And while the predominant blocks of choreography have remained much the same, line dancers from one region of the country frequently perform a specific line dance slightly different from dancers in another region. So don't be alarmed if you find the dances I describe here aren't quite the same way you remember learning them—they're just a variation on the standard.

FOOTWORK

It is difficult to describe the footwork of line dances as it varies from dance to dance. However, the one thing to keep in mind is that all line dances

are performed on flexible knees, never locked, because of the quick shifts in body weight from one foot to the other.

TIMING AND RHYTHM

Almost all songs to which line dances are performed are written in 4/4 timing with steps and dance moves set in groups of 8 counts. The entire choreography of some line dances has only 16 steps and 16 counts of music. Others consist of 16 to 32 steps danced to as many as 42 counts of music.

DANCE PATTERN BUILDING BLOCKS

One of the reasons why line dances are so much fun is because they're primarily made up of groups of forward and back walking steps, of triple (shuffle) steps danced in all directions and of rocking steps all of which are easy to learn and to perform. There are also a series of traditional dance moves like grapevines, lock steps, stomps and swivels which are shared by many line dances, although each combined in different forms.

The most common choreography dance blocks in line dances are:

Grapevine

A Grapevine consists of a sequence of three steps that travel from side to side with one foot crossing behind the other.

Step	Foot Placement
1	Sd with RF
2	Cross LF behind RF
3	Sd with RF
	(Reverse direction)
4	Sd with LF
5	Cross RF behind LF
6	Sd with LF

Step 1.

Step 2.

Step 3.

Heel-Toe Swivels

In order to learn and practice this move, place your feet about 10 inches apart. Keep your knees in a bent position and the weight of your body over the front of the feet.

How to do a toe-in swivel:

Keeping your weight over the front part of your feet, move your heels outward letting your toes move toward each other.

How to do a toe-out swivel:

Maintaining your weight over the front part of your feet, move your heels inward toward each other.

Starting position.

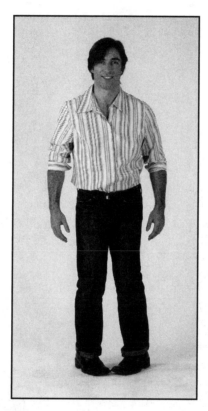

Toe-in swivel.

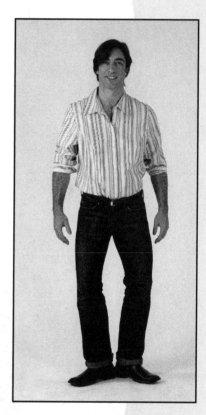

Toe-out swivel.

Taps

In country western dancing, tap steps can be performed with either the heels or the toes to the front of the body, to the sides of the body, across the front of the body, or across the back of the body.

A front-toe tap.

A front-heel tap.

A side-toe tap.

An across the back-toe tap.

A side-heel tap.

Scuff

In a scuff the dancer brushes the heel of one foot on the floor. Scuffs are always done as the dancer moves in a straight forward line.

Stomps

In a stomp the dancer lifts a foot off the dance floor than places it back on the floor without shifting weight onto it.

Scuff.

Stomp.

Locks

In a lock the dancer is moving forward with one foot then crosses the other foot behind the first moving foot, shifting weight onto it.

Hip Bumps and Grinds

During hip bumps and grinds the dancer stands with feet apart and knees bent switching his weight from one foot to the other by moving his hips to the right or to the left.

Locks.

Hip bumps and grinds.

Chassé

A chassé is a sequence of three forward, back or side steps. The cha-cha triple step is a chassé move.

Swivels and Pivots

In both a swivel and a pivot the dancer rotates his body on the weight-bearing foot 1/4 to 1/2 to the left or to the right.

CHARACTERISTIC STYLING

Here again there are no set styling characteristics as line dances are performed individually in large groups. Because line dances involve movements of the feet and body rather than of the arms, except when hands are brought together for an accented clap, many dancers will go through an entire dance with their hands placed on the sides of their waist or with each of their thumbs placed inside their belt.

Country Line Dance Pattern No. 1

The Tush Push

This dance is also often called the Achy Breaky because it was choreographed to Bill Ray Cyrus's rendition of that song. But it can be danced to just about any medium tempo country western song.

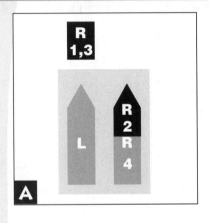

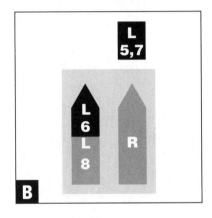

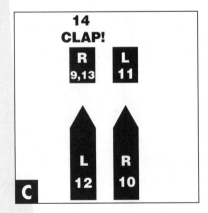

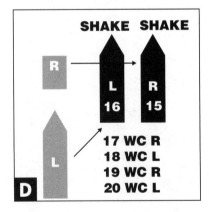

Country Line Dance Pattern No. 1

The Tush Push

Box	Step	Count	M & W—Foot Placement
BLOCK NO. 1: HEEL–TOE TAPS			
A	1	1	Tap the R heel in front of the LF
	2	2	Tap the R toe next to the LF
	3	3	Tap the R heel in front of the LF
	4	4	Close the RF to the LF (WC)
B	5	5	Tap the L heel in front of the RF
	6	6	Tap the L toe next to the RF
	7	7	Tap the L heel in front of the RF
	8	8	Close the LF to the RF (WC)
C	9	9	Tap the R heel in front of the LF
	10	&	Close the RF to the LF (WC)
	11	10	Tap the L heel in front of the RF
	12	&	Close the LF to the RF (WC)
	13	11	Tap the R heel in front of the LF
	14	12	Hold the position and clap your hands
BLOCK NO. 2: HIP BUMPS			
D	15	1 & 2	Step Sd with RF. Shake R hip twice to R
	16	3 & 4	Step Sd with LF. Shake L hip twice to L
	17	5	Shake hips to R
	18	6	Shake hips to L
	19	7	Shake hips to R
	20	8	Shake hips to L

Country Line Dance Pattern No. 1

The Tush Push

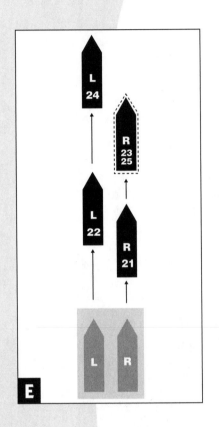

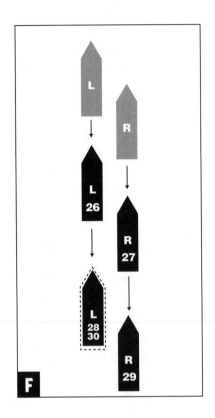

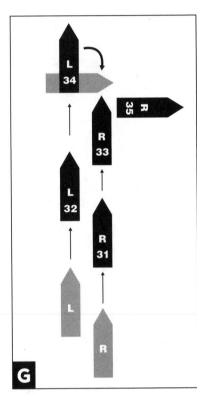

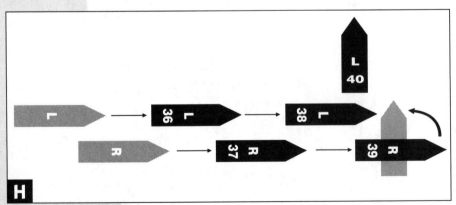

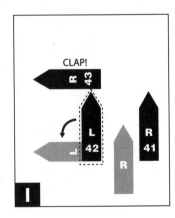

Country Line Dance Pattern No. 1

The Tush Push

Box	Step	Count	M & W—Foot Placement
BLOCK NO. 3: TRIPLE CHASSÉ			
E	21	1	Fwd with RF
	22	&	Fwd with LF
	23	2	Fwd with RF
	24	3	Fwd with LF (forward rock/break move)
	25	4	Bk In-Pl with RF
F	26	5	Bk with LF
	27	&	Bk with RF
	28	6	Bk with LF
	29	7	Bk with RF (back rock/break move)
	30	8	Fwd In-Pl with LF
G	31	1	Fwd with RF
	32	&	Fwd with LF
	33	2	Fwd with RF
	34	3	Step Fwd with LF and pivot 1/2 to the R
	35	4	Step Fwd with RF
H	36	5	Fwd with LF
	37	&	Fwd with RF
	38	6	Fwd with LF
	39	7	Step Fwd with RF and pivot 1/2 to the L
	40	8	Step Fwd with LF
I	41	1	Make a small side step to the R with RF
	42	2	Step Sd In-Pl with LF and swivel 1/4 to the L
	43	3	Close RF to LF (WC)
		4	Clap your hands

Repeat four times to end up facing the same wall you faced at the start of the dance.

Country Line Dance Pattern No. 2

Boot Scootin' Boogie

The original version of this line dance was choreographed by Bill Bader in 1990. Today it remains one of the most popular line dances worldwide. However, its popularity has also resulted in numerous variations and adaptations some of which don't even resemble the original. This version is one I learned in Texas and then saw again being danced in Florida. But, again, dancers beware of regional variations.

Toe-Out Swivel.

Toe-Heel Swivels (Left).

Toe-Heel Swivels (Right).

Country Line Dance Pattern No. 2

Boot Scootin' Boogie

Box	Step	Count	M & W—Foot Placement
BLOCK NO. 1: TOE-HEEL SWIVELS DANCED TO THE RIGHT AND TO THE LEFT SIDES			
Start with feet slightly apart and with weight on the LF			
A	1	1	Swivel R toe outward
	2	2	Swivel R toe inward
	3	3	Swivel R toe outward
	4	4	Swivel R toe in, shifting weight onto the balls of both feet
B	5	5	Swivel toes 1/8 to the L, moving both heels 1/8 to the R and immediately shift weight back to the balls of the feet.
	6	6	Swivel heels 1/8 to the L, moving both toes 1/8 to the R and immediately shift weight back to the heels of the feet
	7	7	Swivel toes 1/8 to the L, moving both heels 1/8 to the R and immediately shift weight back to the toes of both feet
	8	8	TAP the left heel to the side of the RF
C	9	9	Shift the weight onto the toes of the LF swiveling toes 1/8 to the R
	10	10	Swivel the heels of both feet 1/8 to the L, immediately shifting the weight onto the toes.
	11	11	Swivel the toes of both feet 1/8 to the R, immediately shifting the weight onto the LF
	12	12	TAP the RF diagonally to the side of the LF

Country Line Dance Pattern No. 2

Boot Scootin' Boogie

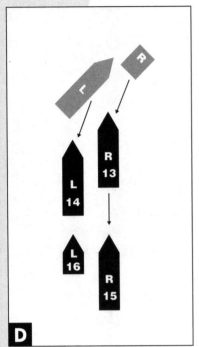

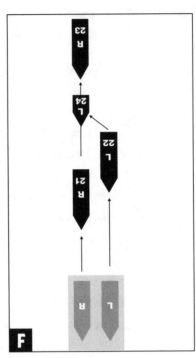

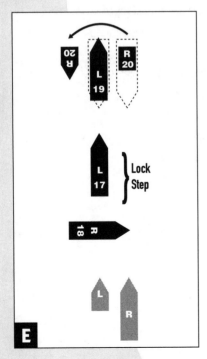

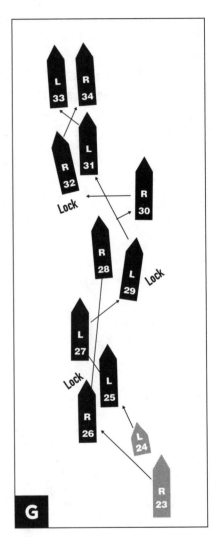

Continuous Lock Steps.

Country Line Dance Pattern No. 2

Boot Scootin' Boogie

Box	Step	Count	M & W—Foot Placement
BLOCK NO. 2: Back and Forward Walk with Lock and Scuff			
D	13	13	Bk with RF
	14	14	Bk with LF
	15	15	Bk with RF
	16	16	Kick the LF Fwd (You can also make this a TAP step)
E	17	17	Fwd with LF
	18	18	Cross RF behind LF (Lock step)
	19	19	Fwd with LF
	20	20	Scuff the floor with the Heel of the R foot then pivot 1/2 Trn to your Left on your LF, bringing the R knee to the side of the Left knee
F	21	21	Bk with RF
	22	22	Bk with LF
	23	23	Bk with RF
	24	24	Kick or Tap the LF in front of the RF
BLOCK NO. 3 : Left and Right Traveling Grapevines with Locks			
G	25	25	Step diagonally forward and to the L with LF
	26	26	Cross RF behind LF (Lock step)
	27	27	Step diagonally forward and to the L with LF
	28	28	Step diagonally forward and to the R with RF
	29	29	Cross LF behind RF (Lock step)
	30	30	Step diagonally forward and to the R with RF
	31	31	Step diagonally forward and to the L with LF
	32	32	Cross RF behind LF (Lock step)
	33	33	Step diagonally forward and to the L with LF
	34	34	Close RF to LF without shifting weight. Clap Hands

Chapter 16

Party Line Dances

Although the line dance is often thought of as primarily a country western phenomenon, there are a few very popular line dances performed to rock and pop tunes. The advent of the music video certainly has made these dances easier to teach to a wide audience!

Unlike most country western line dances, party line dances are generally shorter in duration, consist of moves fashioned after simple, everyday-type moves and call for little if any output of energy. In other words, they're not as much about dancing as they are about a group of people having fun at a party. And while I couldn't bring myself to include such all-time party dances like "The Chicken Dance," "The Egyptian" or even "The Twist," I knew this book could not be completed without my featuring the two party dances that, to my everlasting amazement, are still the most popular line dances ever: the Electric Slide and the Macarena.

FOOTWORK

It is difficult to describe the footwork of line dances as it varies from dance to dance. However, the one thing to keep in mind is that all line dances are performed on flexible knees, never locked, because of the quick shifts in body weight from one foot to the other.

TIMING AND RHYTHM

All line dances are performed to individual musical counts per foot or body movement. The choreography of line dances seldom ever stick to the musical phrasing of the song they are performed to. Some line dances are completed in 16 counts of music. Others take as many as 42 counts of music.

DANCE PATTERN BUILDING BLOCKS

Line dances consist of sequences of mostly standard dance moves that have been linked together. Line dances are also called "wall" dances because they are choreographed with dancers facing one wall and then moving counterclockwise from wall to wall. Some line dances are two wall dances. A few are four-wall dances.

The most common choreography dance blocks in line dances are:

Hip Bumps and Grinds

During hip bumps and grinds the dancer stands with feet apart and knees bent switching his weight from one foot to the other by moving his hips to the right or to the left.

Grapevine

A Grapevine consists of a sequence of three steps that travel from side to side with one foot crossing behind the other.

Step	Foot Placement
1	Sd with RF
2	Cross LF behind RF
3	Sd with RF
	(Reverse direction)
4	Sd with LF
5	Cross RF behind LF
6	Sd with LF

Swivels and Pivots

In both a swivel and a pivot the dancer rotates his body on the weight-bearing foot 1/4 to 1/2 to the left or to the right.

CHARACTERISTIC STYLING

Here again there are no set styling characteristics as line dances are performed individually in large groups. But line dances set to rock and pop tunes tend to use more arm movements than country line dances and also often borrow the Latin hip motion to give the dance a little more sass.

Party Line Dance Pattern No. 1

The Electric Slide

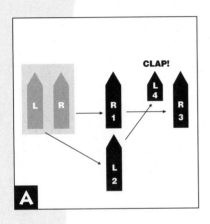

A

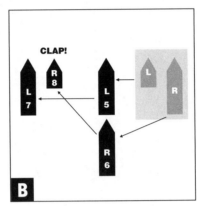

B

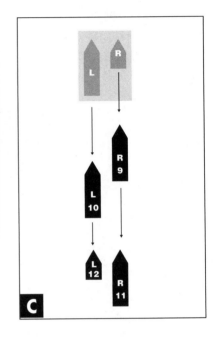

C

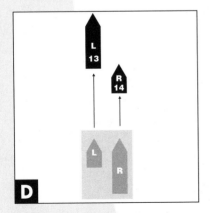

D

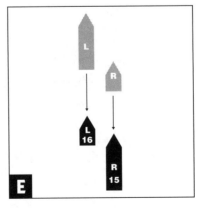

E

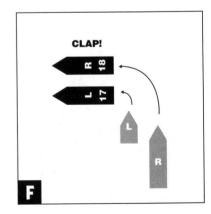

F

Party Line Dance Pattern No. 1

The Electric Slide

A four wall dance, the Electric Slide is the most performed line dance there is. It consists of simple, standard, dance moves like grapevines, walks and lunges which can be easily performed by people of all ages. Over the years, I've seen so many variations of this dance that chances are a few of them don't even resemble the original, whose creator is a matter of some ongoing dispute. What follows is the simplest version of it that I know. It is also one that I've seen danced by kids as well as by adults all over the world for a number of years. In addition to the diagram, see the photos on the following pages illustrating the dance.

Box	Step	Count	M & W—Foot Placement
BLOCK NO. 1: GRAPEVINE TO THE RIGHT AND TO THE LEFT			
Variations of this move include syncopated side steps to right and left, and turns to right and left.			
A	1	1	Step to the R with RF
	2	2	Cross LF directly behind the RF
	3	3	Step to the R with RF
	4	4	Tap or Kick the LF and clap your hands
B	5	5	Step to the L with LF
	6	6	Cross RF directly behind the LF
	7	7	Step to the L with LF
	8	8	Tap of Kick the RF and clap your hands
BLOCK NO. 2: BACK WALK AND ROCK LUNGES			
C	9	9	Step Bk with RF
	10	10	Step Bk with LF
	11	11	Step Bk with RF
	12	12	Tap or Kick LF directly in front of RF
D	13	13	Rock or Lunge forward with LF
	14	14	Tap RF behind LF
E	15	15	Step Bk with RF
	16	16	Tap LF in front of RF
F	17	17	Step Fwd on LF pivoting 1/4 to L
	18	18	Close RF to LF without shifting weight and clap your hands

Party Line Dance Pattern No. 1

The Electric Slide

DANCE TIP:

The photographs show the mirror opposite of what you are doing.

Party Line Dance Pattern No. 1

The Electric Slide

Clap!

Clap!

Party Line Dance Pattern No.1

The Electric Slide

Party Line Dance Pattern No.1

The Electric Slide

Clap.

Party Line Dance Pattern No. 2

The Macarena

In 1993 a Spanish singing duo, Los del Rio, released a song called "Macarena." To my knowledge, an unknown choreographer created a series of hand moves to accompany the lyrics of the song. Little did he or she or Los del Rio themselves imagined that both the song and its moves would sweep across the entire world at the speed of sound, or that they would see their work being performed by thousands of baseball fans in Yankee Stadium. Although I still have a problem with calling it "a dance," even a "line dance," I can't help smiling every time I do it or every time I see people of all ages do it.

There are sixteen hand moves to the Macarena. Each of them is performed while the hips move from side to side.

Party Line Dance Pattern No. 2

The Macarena

Box	Count	Move
1	1	Extend your right arm forward. Palm of hand facing downward
2	2	Extend your left arm forward. Palm of hand facing downward
3	3	Turn the palm of your right hand upwards
4	4	Turn the palm of your left hand upwards
5	5	Place the palm of your right hand over the inside of your left elbow
6	6	Place the palm of your left hand over the inside of your right elbow
7	7	Place the palm of your right hand over your right ear
8	8	Place the palm of your left hand over your left ear
9	9	Place the palm of your right hand across the body and over your left hip
10	10	Place the palm of your left hand across the body and over your right hip
11	11	Place the palm of your right hand behind your right hip
12	12	Place the palm of your left hand behind your left hip
13	13	Move your right hip to the right
14	14	Move your left hip to the left
15	15	Move your right hip to the right
16	16	Hop on your left foot, turning 1/4 to your left and clap your hands

Are you smiling, too?

Party Line Dance Pattern No. 2

The Macarena

1

2

5

6

Party Line Dance Pattern No. 2

The Macarena

Party Line Dance Pattern No. 2

The Macarena

9

10

13

14

Party Line Dance Pattern No. 2

The Macarena

Conclusion

During the late thirties and forties, Fred Astaire personified not only the formality of ballroom dancing with his legendary top hat and tails, but also the seamless execution of his partnering moves. The smoothness, musicality, and control of Fred Astaire's body and footwork—the elegance he exuded with his various dancing partners—made him the sort of man women dreamt of dancing with and men wished they could dance like. He made it all look so easy, so natural.

Amazingly, it's been reported that Mr. Astaire never considered himself a ballroom dancer, but a dancer who loved the partnership element of ballroom-style dancing. It's been likewise reported that Mr. Astaire often said that he had never met a so-called "natural" dancer, that all the dancers he knew took lessons and practiced all the time. Articles regarding the many days and long hours of rehearsal with his dance partners before filming abound.

Today, ballroom dancing has evolved into several styles, levels of proficiency, and worldwide competitive events. The artistry of the performances and dance routines that we see on televised dance competitions, like those shown on PBS, are but one example. Yet, I know that anyone who's ever watched this event, including nondancers, can see that the performance of the vast majority of competitors includes moves and techniques from various forms of dance, such as ballet, modern, and jazz dance.

While at such top levels of dance performance it is often difficult to recognize any of the fundamental elements of social style, partner dancing or, even, of intermediate levels of ballroom dancing, I can guarantee you that every one of those wonderful competitors started by learning how to take a forward step, then a box step, or by learning how to hold a dance partner, or even by picking up a book or a video in order to learn a couple of dance steps for a party or a wedding.

The main objective of this book has been to provide you with just enough instruction and information about partner dancing to get you on the dance floor. Once you do, I guarantee you'll want to continue to learn more about dancing. It's a wonderful thing to be able to do.

Keep on dancing.
Cal Pozo

Abbreviations and Dance Terms

A: Apart

&: And. Meaning 1/2 a count of music per individual foot placement.

BF: Ball/Foot

BK: Back

CBM: Contra Body Motion. A gradual twisting of the upper torso in the direction you plan to lead a closed dance position turn.

CL: Closed Dance Position

Close: The traveling foot steps next to the supporting foot and a change of weight takes place.

DP: Dance Position

Fwd: Forward

HL: Heel Lead

Hold: When dancers do not move during a beat of music, as in the waltz. Also referred to as a hesitation.

Holds:

1HH: One-Hand Hold

2HH: Two-Hand Hold

XHH: Cross-Hand Hold

In-Pl: In Place. This means that you should take your foot off the dance floor and then place it back in the same place. Often used describing rock/break foot placements.

LF: Left Foot

LO: Left Open

LOD: Line of Dance. The counterclockwise direction in which couples move when dancing a smooth dance.

LS: Left Side

NWC: No Weight Change. One foot is closing to the other foot, but no change of weight occurs.

O: Open. When partners break dance position.

Pivot: A pivot is both a body movement and a foot action. The body rotates left or right while standing on one foot. Pivots range in movement between 1/4 to 1/2 turns.

Q: Quick. When a single foot movement is danced to one beat of music.

RF: Right Foot

RO: Right Open

RS: Right Side

S: Slow. When a single foot movement is danced to 2 beats of music.

Sd: Side

Spin: A full 360-degree turn performed on one foot.

Swivel: A swivel is also a body movement and a foot action. The body rotates left or right while standing on one or both feet. Swivels range in movement between 1/8 to 1/4 turns. A swivel can be done with just the heel, keeping the weight of the swiveling foot on the ball of theat foot, or it can be done with just the toe, keeping the weight of the swiveling foot on the heel.

TT: Toe Tap. The toe of one foot taps on the floor.

Trn: Turn

UA: Underarm

WC: Weight Change. The body's weight changes from one foot to the other foot.

X: Cross

Index of Dance Patterns

Waltz Dance Patterns

Foxtrot Dance Patterns

Tango Dance Patterns

DANCE PATTERN #	NAME	PAGE NUMBER
1	The Tango Basic A	86
2	The Tango Basic B (Left Open)	88
3	Rock and Corté Lunge	90

Rumba Dance Patterns

DANCE PATTERN #	NAME	PAGE NUMBER
1	The Closed Box Step	110
2	The Turning Box Step	112
3	The Fifth Position Breaks	114
4	The Underarm Turn	118
5	The Cross Body Lead	122

Salsa Dance Patterns

DANCE PATTERN #	NAME	PAGE NUMBER
1	Forward and Back Breaks	138
2	Side-to-Side Breaks	140
3	The Open Break	142
4	The Progressive Basic	144
5	The Cross Body Lead	146
6	The Underarm Turn	148

Cha-cha Dance Patterns

DANCE PATTERN #	NAME	PAGE NUMBER
1	The Side Basic	160
2	The Progressive Basic	162
3	The Open Break	164
4	The Underarm Turn	166
5	The Cross Overs	170

Merengue Dance Patterns

DANCE PATTERN #	NAME	PAGE NUMBER
1	The Eight Count Basic	178
2	Forward and Back Walks (Passing the Feet)	180
3	Forward and Back Walks (Closing the Feet)	182

Swing Dance Patterns

Dance Pattern #	Name	Page Number
1	Triple-Step Swing Basic A	194
2	Triple-Step Swing Basic B	196
3	Triple-Step Swing Basic C (Left Turning Basic)	198
4	The Open Break	200
5	The Underarm Turn	202
6	The Reverse Underarm Turn	204
7	The Double Reverse Underarm Turn	206

Hustle Dance Patterns

Dance Pattern #	Name	Page Number
1	The Basic Time Step	212
2	Changing Places	214
3	Reverse Loop Turn	216
4	Hustle Whip	218

Country Line Dance Patterns

Dance Pattern #	Name	Page Number
1	The Tush Push	230
2	Boot Scootin' Boogie	234

Party Line Dance Patterns

Dance Pattern #	Name	Page Number
1	The Electric Slide	242
2	The Macarena	248

About the Author

Former ballroom dance champion and Broadway dancer/choreographer, Cal Pozo is a fitness author and the award-winning producer/director/choreographer of multiple popular dance and fitness DVDs. His production credits include the works of fitness personalities Denise Austin, Kathy Smith, Leslie Sansone, and the cast of TV reality shows like *The Biggest Loser* and *Dancing With the Stars*. He is also the host of several DVDs, including "Learning to Dance in Minutes," "DanceFit," and "Partner Dancing 101."